What's Happening in Our Family?

What's Happening in Our Family?

Understanding Sexual Abuse Through Metaphors

Constance M. Ostis, MSW

Safer Society Press
PO BOX 340 • BRANDON • VT 05733

Author's note: *While every effort has been made to identify original sources, it is likely that some portions of this book convey ideas and concepts neither original to the author or attributed to anyone else. After 15 years of work in the field of sexual abuse treatment, I have assimilated and integrated many concepts that have become part of common practice. It has been difficult in some situations to discern or recall original authorship. To all the many experts in the field from whom I have learned, I give my deepest thanks and request your understanding if I have not given credit where it is due. Just as I hope that others will pick up the ideas conveyed in this book and make them their own, I trust that other authors will understand how I took on these ideas and unwittingly made them my own. All our efforts together, however, serve the same purpose: to convey knowledge and understanding that helps make this world a safer place for children.*

Editor: Euan Bear, Mountain Bear Services
Interior design and composition: Jenna Dixon, Bookbuilder
Illustrations: Greg Crawford
Copyeditor: Linda Lotz
Proofreader: Beth Richards

Printed in the United States of America by Malloy Lithographing, Inc.

⊗ The paper used is this publication meets the minimum requirements of the American National Standard for Information Sciences — Permanence of Paper for Printed Library Materials, ANSI Z39.48-1984.

ISBN 1-884444-65-2 / $20.00 / Bulk discounts available.

Order from:

Safer Society Press
PO Box 340, Brandon VT 05733

To receive a catalog or to place a phone order with your Visa or MasterCard, please call 802-247-3132.

Library of Congress Cataloging-in-Publication Data

Ostis, Constance M., 1943–
    What's happening in our family? : understanding sexual abuse through metaphors / Constance M. Ostis.
       p. cm.
    Includes bibliographical references.
    ISBN 1-884444-65-2 (alk. paper)
    1. Incest—Psychological aspects. 2. Incest victims—Counseling of. 3. Family psychotherapy. 4. Family social work. 5. Metaphor—Therapeutic use. I. Title.
    HV6570.6 .O88 2002
    362.76'86—dc21   2001057829

10 09 08 07 06 05 04 03 02 01   10 9 8 7 6 5 4 3 2 1   1st printing 2002

contents

....

Foreword, by Jan Hindman   vii

Acknowledgments   ix

Introduction   1

Part One   Looking at Sexual Abuse in the Family   11

Section I: Understanding Sexual Abuse   13

1   What Exactly Is Sexual Abuse?   13

2   Abuser or Victim: "That's Not All I Am!"   19

Section II: Understanding the Sexual Abuser   27

3   Finding Out What the Abuser Did   27

4   It's a Puzzle: Why Do Abusers Do It?   30

5   Sexual Abuse Is a Hard-to-Stop, Complicated Problem   39

Section III: Understanding the Abused Child in the Family   50

6   Why Abusers Choose Particular Children   50

7   Who's to Blame?   61

8   Why the Whole Family Comes for Treatment:
Abuse Is Everybody's Problem   65

Part Two   How Much Harm?   77

9   Recognizing the Hidden Injury   79

10   Child Sexual Abuse Is More than a Family Problem:
It's a Crime   85

11   Assessment of Trauma and Other Injuries: Why the Whole Family
Can't Be Together for a While   92

12   When Supervised Visitation Makes Sense   96

Part Three   Longer Stories About Secret Behavior in the Family   103

13 "Stealing the Family Cookies": A Story of Adult Manipulation   105

14 "Borrowing the Family Car": A Story of Youthful Manipulation   120

Part Four   Treatment and Restitution   135

15 Thinking About Treatment: Repairing the Hidden Hurt   137

16 Selecting Treatment: The Need for Specialized Counseling   140

17 Treatment for Abused Children: Victims and Siblings   143

18 Treatment for Nonabusing Parents and Families: Regaining a Power Balance   152

19 Treatment for Abusers   157

20 Surviving Treatment: Coping with Painful Emotions   176

Part Five   Remain Separate or Reunify: Making the Best Decision for Your Family   183

21 Should Your Family Get Back Together?   185

22 Less than the Whole Truth: Conditions that Make Family Reunification Unsafe   188

23 Looking for the End of Treatment: It's a Long and Winding Road 193

Appendix A   Differences in Power: Factors to Consider when Children Interact Sexually   201

Appendix B   Assessment Guidelines   203

About the Author   209

About Safer Society Press   210

foreword

....

The idea that children are usually sexually abused by someone they know, often by a family member, is unthinkable. It is not only families who struggle to recognize that indeed sexual abuse most often happens in families; the rampant reality of family sexual abuse also approaches the door of traditionally trained clinicians with a rude knock. Although well-intentioned, these same therapists often tackle this problem through training dedicated to "deep-dish" psychotherapy methods for treating any problem and thus are unprepared to work with families in which sexual abuse has occurred. What they may lack is language and knowledge of how to connect and work with families and help them understand what has occurred. Too often the language of thickly bound textbooks, graduate school programs, and psychotherapy training centers discusses child sexual abuse within a complicated framework that focuses on theoretical understandings of causes of abuse, dysfunctional arousal patterns, recidivism rates, or sensational cases of child murder and abduction.

Author and social worker Connie Ostis understands the potential for confusion and severe emotional stress on the part of families, as well as for distress and uncertainty on the part of many therapists searching for a way to talk with these families. To address both concerns, she has created a valuable resource in *What's Happening in Our Family?* Her unique approach demystifies the problem of family sexual abuse and allows the use of illustrated metaphor and everyday language to assist both families and clinicians on the road to healing the wounds of incest. Ms. Ostis writes with understanding and compassion as she addresses many of the problems common to families who so desperately need to break through denial, abandon traditional thought, and work together.

What's Happening in Our Family? reflects an awareness that when sexual abuse emerges in a family, the whole family can be badly hurt. The healing process requires some type of language and method that responds to the needs of all family members — adults, adolescents, and children. As Connie Ostis recognizes, the use of creative stories, metaphors, and ordinary examples is one effective way to establish a mutually trusting relationship with family members, to break down barriers of resistance, and to make clear the path to healing. The delightfully soft but extremely powerful technique of story is less confrontational and easier to hear for a family confused and shocked by the devastating reality of "it happened in our family." This book is written in non-jargon, everyday language that is easily understandable and sends a strong message of healing for all members of the family.

Ms. Ostis demonstrates a sensitivity for the emotional upheaval that can engulf a family when sexual abuse is disclosed. With *What's Happening in Our Family?* she offers family members a way to break through the invisible wall of grief that often locks them into narrow ways of thinking about the problem. She provides clinicians with a valuable resource to help these families heal their emotional pain and create future safety in the family. Connie Ostis emphasizes the importance of the family in the victim's recovery and stresses the importance of the entire family rightly placing appropriate responsibility upon the abuser. She also encourages the family to make important decisions about whether or not they get back together.

This easy-to-read book provides a way for both family members and clinicians to approach this hard-to-discuss topic. While the book gives family members information to increase their understanding and help them break through denial, it is written in a manner to convey empathy and support. *What's Happening in Our Family?* not only furnishes clinicians with unique tools, it also provides a strong message of hope for the emotional and psychological recovery of the family who makes a commitment to change and who may one day return to an environment of trust and safety.

Jan Hindman

author of *A Very Touching Book: For Little People and Big People*

acknowledgments

I extend my heartfelt thanks to the clients, the clinicians, the support staff, and the administrators of Community Counseling Center in Portland, Maine, and to the Board of Directors and executive director Henry Nielsen for providing a writing sabbatical. Also thanks to former clinical director Sylvia Schroeder for her encouragement and early review. Steve Beaudette and Maryann Wilson helped me through a state of computer anxiety.

All members of the Sexual Abuse Treatment Team, past and present, responded enthusiastically and eagerly incorporated metaphor into their own work. Cate Nyary first suggested a book. Colleagues Rita Nugent and Jeannie Giberson made invaluable contributions and, along with Sheila McKinley, Jackie Lepine Johnson, and Vicki Piper Kendrick, critically read my manuscript. Michael Graff helped produce a video of a metaphorical story. Others gave feedback on metaphor use in a psychoeducational group setting: Janice Travers, Marlene Kane, Ellen Gurney, and David May. Robbie Lipsman provided a much-needed nonclinical perspective.

I am grateful to others outside the agency who also took the time to review the manuscript: therapists Carol Lohman, Mary Maescher, and Tracy Morton Stanford and writer and friend Pat Nyhan. Cumberland County Child Abuse and Neglect Council director Lucky Hollander provided a valuable critique of the manuscript. Several persons from the Department of Human Services gave positive feedback: Valerie Meserve on her use of the metaphor video with families, and Karen Westberg and Sandy Hodge on my use of these metaphors in training interns and staff. Many colleagues reported enhanced understanding of concepts following a presentation of some of these metaphors at a statewide judicial symposium.

This book would not have been possible without the enthusiastic support of all members of my family, particularly my children, Jay, Nathan, and Lauren, and my husband, Harry, who gave hours to critically reading the manuscript. From my parents, Jack and Jean Smith, I received a deep appreciation for the importance of a caring, safe family and the belief that no matter how hard a problem is, the only way through it is to do something about it. My sisters Sarah and Jennie provided much needed emotional support. Friends Pat and Chris Nyhan, C. L. and Ione Townsend, Betsy and Ozzie Wales, and Mary Taber helped me keep perspective in life and understood when I needed to put friendship time on hold.

While I have drawn on the work of many, my commitment to the field of child sexual abuse has been most profoundly influenced by Jan Hindman. I also thank my professors: Sophie Freud for her general inspiration, Helen Reinhertz and Abbie Frost for supporting my vision of a dissertation on metaphor, and Cathy Siebold for her clarity on the application of this manuscript to a curriculum format. Above all, I am exceedingly grateful for the solid editing skills, reassurance, and caring of my editor Euan Bear for Safer Society Foundation and Press.

It was primarily through the process of listening to clients and learning from their responses that I found the language for developing metaphors and learned when metaphors work, and when they don't. One couple critiqued this manuscript a year after completing treatment and stated: "I wish there had been something like this when we started. We looked everywhere for something written in a way that we could understand." Another couple, through interviews with the abusing parent and consultation with the nonabusing parent, inspired the web-metaphor conceptualization of a holistic relapse prevention plan.

I have worked as a social worker for over 30 years, almost half that time in the field of child sexual abuse. I have developed great respect for the ways people cope with painful childhoods and difficult adulthoods. And I have been sincerely touched by the commitment many families make to the hard work of change and to the repair of hidden harm caused by sexual abuse. It is to the people who allowed me into their lives and enriched my own that I give my deepest gratitude.

introduction

....

An Invitation to Professionals Working with Families Dealing with Sexual Abuse

The challenge in all meaningful human relationships is to establish bonds that promote understanding, caring, and support. That hurdle at times feels insurmountable for family members and professionals coming together around the problem of sexual abuse within families. Both professionals and family members come to the work with their own apprehensions and preconceptions. In the child protection and legal realm, family members often experience a tremendous loss of their life as they once knew it. They cope with a wide range of emotions as they try to come to terms with what has occurred. At the same time they feel understandably disempowered and sometimes blamed as a phalanx of professionals investigates and otherwise invasively examines their lives. In the therapeutic setting, family members are often unprepared to trust the people to whom they have come for help; therapists are often ill prepared to converse with the very people to whom they are offering services.

What both clients and therapists have in common, however, is their concern about the impact that the disclosure of sexual abuse has on children and on the family as a whole. What is often lacking in the professional relationship, with those whose role is defined as either protective or therapeutic, is a medium through which everyone can talk in the same language as they work together to discover what happened, why it happened, what harm has resulted, and how to prevent sexual abuse from occurring again.

I have written *What's Happening in Our Family?* for direct use by the general public and by clients in treatment. Many professionals have indicated they found the contents useful for grasping concepts and developing a non-jargon way to talk with families troubled with sexual abuse. I encourage my therapeutic and social work colleagues to use this book in both ways— directly with clients and for their own professional development in finding a new, more communicative vocabulary that works with their clients.

The support of their nonabusing parent or parents is one of the strongest factors in determining how abused children resolve trauma related to their abuse[1] and whether sexually reactive children[2] or sexually abusing adolescents[3] and adults become responsible for their behaviors and their work in treatment.[4] Yet parental ability to provide this much-needed support is often hampered by their own emotional upheaval and by the subsequent erosion of their social support system: disclosure of sexual abuse in the family threatens their connection to the community as well as to their extended family.

Over the past 15 years as supervisor of a sexual abuse treatment program, I have developed the metaphor-based language represented in *What's Happening in Our Family?* presented within both therapeutic and psychoeducational contexts. Metaphor bridges the communication gap between client and clinician and provides support for the therapeutic task of promoting healing.[5] While the therapist offers a metaphor as one means of conveying significant information, it is the client who takes the metaphor in to make meaning of his or her own unique situation. The metaphors presented here grew instinctively out of a need to find a way to speak about the unspeakable: child sexual abuse.

Interest in developing the use of metaphor in therapy and in psychoeducational sessions became a turning point in my work in the field of sexual abuse. The use of metaphor with clients, with new trainees, and with other professionals in the community seemed to bring clarity to the very difficult concepts of subtle coercion, hidden agendas, irresponsibility, power, victim-blaming, violation of trust, personal boundaries, and thinking errors, among others, that are involved in sexual abuse. Metaphors seemed particularly useful for helping parents "get it." By looking at a parallel situation in a nonsexual metaphor, parents could first externalize the problem outside of themselves, set aside their resistance, and more willingly enter the hard work of therapy. Once engaged, they seemed more open to reflecting on their own issues and contemplating the changes necessary to ensure their children's safety in the future.

The metaphors were created at various times with many different clients. But each time one came to mind, it evolved from the collaborative dialogue of the session and with the language of the client in mind. I would like to suggest that you use these metaphors, as well as some of your own creation, as I do—not only to convey conceptual information but also to convey empathy and support as you work to strengthen your relationship with your clients. Whenever I speak in language that both the client and I understand, the relationship becomes more meaningful, and the goals of treatment become more definable. You might recommend to some clients that they read the whole book, but for many others, you might find it more useful to simply use the language and stories presented in each section to aid you in your therapeutic conversations. You may choose to use different sections of *What's Happening in Our Family?* in a different order than presented, or to use only certain parts in session. Many sections could be particularly useful in talking with children, either individually or in family sessions. Metaphor, already part of everyday language, can be part of treatment, thus becoming a vehicle of communication, not only between therapists and parents but also between these parents and their children.

Helping families cope with and heal from the effects of sexual abuse is important work, requiring a continuing sense of hope for change and a belief in resilience. Families come to treatment laden with a disconnection in their life narrative: the old story about themselves and how they perceived their lives has been disrupted by the abuse and its disclosure and the intrusion of outsiders into their lives. Along with this exposure of their private worlds evolves a story about themselves and those they love that does not yet make sense. Families have many questions that need answers before they can put together the disconnected pieces of the past and begin to develop new connections for the future. Helping to change individual and family stories about themselves can be some of the most rewarding work we will ever be fortunate enough to share with our clients. We need all the effective tools we can find to support parents' efforts to understand, believe, and support their children. I offer these metaphors and this book as an addition to your therapist's tool kit, with the hope that they prove as effective in your work as they have in mine.

An Open Letter to Families Dealing with Sexual Abuse

Perhaps you are reading this book because an adult, or an older child, abused a child in your family or in a family you know. Perhaps you are a child who has been sexually abused. Perhaps you are the brother or sister or cousin of the abused child or of the abuser, and you have been worried or frightened by what has been happening in your family. Perhaps you are the spouse or partner of the abuser. You may be the parent of the abuser, the victim, or both. If you just recently learned about the abuse, you may be in a state of shock.

You may be having a very hard time putting all the information together so that it makes any sense at all. You may be having a battle inside yourself. Sometimes you may clearly believe that sexual abuse has occurred, but at other times, you may refuse to believe that it could have happened in your family. Sometimes you believe and strongly support the child who was abused, but at other times, you believe and support the person who did the abusing. The information you are hearing from the abused child and from the abuser may be quite different. The abuser may offer innocent explanations that sound convincing. The child, too, may be quite confused and scared, because telling about the abuse has made everyone so upset.

Perhaps you are reading this book because you are the one who has sexually abused a child. You may have admitted what you did and are very sorry for the harm you have caused others. You may be ready for treatment as you search for answers, or you may think treatment is a waste of time and money. You may believe that your promise to yourself and to your family is enough to keep you from ever abusing again. You may be having a hard time being honest, even with yourself. You may feel deep shame and not want to look at the harm you have done to a child and to your whole family. You may resist taking responsibility for the pain and, instead, join in your family's anger at outside authorities. It is understandable that you might react in so many different ways. You have probably never been in such emotional pain yourself. You have probably never seen your family members so unhappy and frightened about the present, or so unsure of the future.

Each member of a family faces many questions that seem to have no clear answers: "How could sexual abuse have happened in my family?" "Why didn't someone *stop* it?" "Whose *fault* is it?" If you are a parent, perhaps your own childhood was marked by unhappiness and abuse, and you probably wanted to make sure abuse did not happen to your children. So how could someone have abused a member of your family? Doubts, confusion, questions whirl around in your mind. "*Why* did the abuser do this to my child?" "If it's true, wouldn't I have *known*?" "Exactly what *harm* was done?" "Is there a difference in the *amount* of harm, if it's fondling or intercourse?" "Exactly *how* does treatment help?" "Why do we have to be *separated* from the abuser? Now that the abuser has been caught and everyone admits it was wrong, why can't our family just go back to *normal*? I'm sure it won't happen again."

Sexual abuse is not the kind of problem behavior that just "stops happening." If it were that simple, abusers would be able to stop themselves before they abused anyone the first time. Abusers always know that sexual contact with younger children is wrong. That is why they keep it secret. They may think many times, "I won't do it again. This is my last time," but the sexual abuse continues. Maybe the abuser did stop, but only after the child told someone. Perhaps the abuser in your family did not really want to stop or did not know how. Sexual abusers allow this negative use of sex to control their lives in much the same way that alcoholics allow the negative use of alcohol to control their lives.

Specialized treatment offers abusers a chance to learn a way out of this problem behavior and a chance to repair the harm they have caused. Sexual abusers can learn skills that keep them in control of their behavior, instead of their behavior being in control of them. Older children and adolescent abusers can find treatment particularly helpful, as long as their abusing behaviors and attitudes are open to change.

You may already understand a lot about sexual abuse but can't always find the words to talk about it with a therapist, other family members, or especially children. This book is written in simple language to help both children and adults understand complicated information. I've used certain types of stories and comparisons called *metaphors* to help you understand some of the hard parts. Some children can read and understand parts of the book by themselves. For other children it would be better if an older person used the metaphors in their discussions about the problem.

What Are Metaphors?

Metaphors are short comparisons or stories that use parts of something we do understand to help us convey ideas or to better understand something we don't understand. They are teaching stories. We all use metaphors every day. For example, we might say, "Her smile brings happiness to me like a beautiful sunrise brings joy to the morning." Metaphors contain parts that are different from the situations they are describing, but they feel similar. They help us understand better.

The metaphors in this book use nonsexual material to explain some feelings, thoughts, and actions about sexual abuse. By thinking about how hard it is to sort the pieces and put together a 500-piece puzzle, for example, we can understand how hard it is to discover all the pieces and put together an understanding of how someone sexually abused a child.

People have used stories and metaphors since time began to teach others, to share a message, to replace confusion with understanding. By reading about a similar, nonsexual situation, you may be able to put aside some of the confusing feelings that come up around sex. You can concentrate on the task of figuring out what damage has been done and how to make things better.

Understanding may not come quickly or easily. At first, you may find that the more you understand, the more upset and confused you become. Sometimes you may see things clearly, only to find that the next day you are confused again. This is a natural reaction to hearing and trying to accept emotionally painful information.

You may feel as though your family is being torn apart. In order to protect children, authorities in child welfare agencies usually set up rules and guidelines that prevent your family from being together for a while. It is difficult to have so many outside professionals involved in your lives. Yet these people are necessary because there is so much work to do and because their jobs are different. Legal and protective agencies are there to determine the facts of the case. They ask lots of questions to find out what happened. Treatment providers are there to help you find ways to understand and reduce the pain from the often invisible emotional and psychological injuries that sexual abuse can cause in the abused child and in the family.

Coming to Terms

In this book I use terms common to the field of sexual abuse. I refer to a sexually abusing person as an "abuser," regardless of the person's age. I refer to the person responsible for the child, but not directly responsible for the inappropriate or abusive acts, as the "nonabusing parent," even when it's a guardian or aunt or uncle or other relative. I frequently refer to a sexually abused child as a "victim." This way, we can keep clear about which person is responsible for doing the abuse and which person's body and trust have been misused.

These children are *victims* because of what the *abuser* did, but more importantly, these children are also *survivors* because of what is *inside* themselves: an ability to find ways to live in a confusing, nonprotective, abusive situation. The more children are able to release themselves from the power of secret thoughts and feelings about the abuse, the less the feelings will hurt them. The more abused children understand and accept their own innocence, the more they can rebuild their lives and become stronger in their identity as survivors.[6]

Sex is not easy to talk about. Talking about sexual abuse is even more difficult—especially when it happens in your own family. When a stranger abuses a child, both the family and the community are clear about their feelings: they are angry at the perpetrator and offer unconditional support to the abused child. When a family member sexually abuses a child, however, people often are not clear. Feelings of anger and sadness, guilt and shame, blame and betrayal may become confused with feelings of love and loyalty.

It takes a lot of courage to do what you are doing: struggling with thoughts and feelings that come up when a child has been sexually abused. Sometimes you might feel quite alone in this struggle. Just at a time when you need the most support, you may feel like friends and family have disappeared. You may feel judged by others who have no idea how much your family means to you or what you are going through. Or others may be there to offer support, but you are so overwhelmed that you wish you could just hide from the eyes of the community. You may be frightened as you look to a future of emotional stress and possible financial difficulty, and you wonder if life will ever get better again.

I have worked for over 15 years helping families heal from the effects of sexual abuse. I have great respect for the work they do to help their children and all affected family members. I wrote this book with the hope that it will give you support as you search for understanding of how sexual abuse happens, how abuse can hurt all members of a family, and how everyone can work together to make the family a safe place in the future.

New Stories for the Future

Stories are important for learning about many things, including telling about who we are as individuals and in relation to our families. During your treatment, you and your family will be creating new stories about your lives. Instead of a story about a family where abuse is occurring or has occurred, you will be developing new ways of being with one another. You will be building a story about a family who is not afraid to face a problem and learn ways to prevent abuse and keep children safe.

If a family cannot change enough to keep its children safe, even after a lot of treatment, those children can still create new helpful stories to limit the power of the old hurtful stories. For example, children can throw away the stories that others might have told about how they were responsible for their own abuse and create new stories about how wonderful they are and how someone took advantage of them when he or she abused them.[7] And as children learn ways to protect themselves they can replace the old story of feeling powerless with a new story of being more powerful.

The Purpose of This Book

The main purpose of this book is to help you begin thinking in a different way about what has been going on in your family and to help you understand why having the whole family in specialized sexual abuse treatment is so important. But even when it's not possible to get everyone to agree to come for treatment, families can still heal. I do not suggest in this book whether or not a family should stay together. Instead, I hope that reading this book will help you gain a clearer awareness of your own situation and the goals of treatment before you make any major decisions.

You can read this book all at once or a few sections at a time — whatever is most helpful to you. What is important is that you are working toward understanding the emotionally painful and complicated problem of sexual abuse. If you can understand what occurred, how it occurred, and how to prevent sexual abuse in the future, you will be taking a huge step in your family's healing.

Notes

1. Corcoran, J. (1998). In defense of mothers of sexual abuse victims. *Families in Society: The Journal of Contemporary Human Services, 10*, 467–480.

   Everson, M. D., Hunter, W. M., Runyon, D. K., Edelsohn, G. A., & Coulter, M. L. (1989). Maternal support following disclosure of incest. *American Journal of Orthopsychiatry, 59*, 197–206.

   Kendall-Tackett, K., Williams, L., & Finkelhor, D. (1993). Impact of sexual abuse on children: A review and syntheses of recent empirical studies. *Psychological Bulletin, 113*, 164–180.

2. Friedrich, W. N. (1995). *Psychotherapy with sexually abused boys: An integrated approach.* Thousand Oaks, Calif.: Sage.

3. Gil, E. (1995). *A guide for parents of children who molest.* Rockville, Md.: Launch Press.

4. Meinig, M. B., & Bonner, B. L. (1990). Returning the treated sex offender to the family. *Violence Update, 1,* 1–11.

5. Carlsen, M. B. (1998). Metaphor, meaning-making, and metamorphosis. In H. Rosen & K. T. Kuehlwein (Eds.), *Constructing realities: Meaning-making perspectives for psychotherapists* (pp. 337–368). San Francisco: Jossey-Bass.

   Lakoff, G., & Johnson, J. (1979). *Metaphors we live by.* Chicago: University of Chicago Press.

   Martin, J., Cummings, A. L. & Hallberg, E. T. (1992). Therapists' intentional use of metaphor: Memorability, clinical impact, and possible epistemic/motivational functions. *Journal of Consulting and Clinical Psychology, 60,* 143–145.

6. Herman, J. (1992). *Trauma and recovery.* New York: Basic Books.

   Hindman, J. (1989). *Just before dawn.* Ontario, Ore.: AlexAndria Associates.

7. White, M., & Epston, D. (1990). *Narrative means to therapeutic ends.* New York: W. W. Norton.

part one

Looking at Sexual Abuse in the Family

section I: understanding sexual abuse

I

....

What Exactly Is Sexual Abuse?

Trying to understand exactly what makes sexual contact *abusive* can be confusing and particularly difficult to explain to children. Let's think about words we might use to discuss this problem with children.

There is a big difference between a healthy sexual relationship and sexual abuse. A healthy sexual relationship occurs between two people who have *equal ability or power* to decide if they want to be together and what they want to do. This is called a *consenting* relationship.

Sexual abuse occurs whenever one person (called the *abuser*, the *perpetrator*, the *molester*, or the *offender*) takes advantage of (abuses) his or her *position of authority or power* to *require secret* sexual activity by someone (called the *victim* or *the abused child*) who is *smaller, younger,* or *in other ways less powerful*.

Sexual abuse involves the parts of the body that are usually covered up by a bathing suit, but also sometimes the mouth, tongue, fingers, and other objects.

For a girl, there are the breasts and the genital area where her "private parts" are (the vagina and the vulva).

For a boy, there is the genital area where his "private parts" are (penis and testicles).

Sometimes, for either boys or girls, sexual abuse might involve the buttocks (also called the "rear end" or "where you sit down") or the bowel movement area (where your poop comes out of, called the rectum or the anus).

Here are some of the activities that would be called *sexual abuse* when an adult or older child does them with or to a child:

- Showing a child sexual pictures (pornography)
- Showing one's genitals (exhibitionism) to another person
- Watching another person bathe or dress or use the toilet in a sexual way (voyeurism)
- Photographing a nude child
- Fondling (touching or stroking) genitals or masturbating in front of others
- Fondling or masturbating another person
- Forcing a child to fondle or masturbate someone else
- Mouth-to-genital contact (*fellatio*, when the mouth is on the penis; *cunnilingus*, when the mouth is on the vagina; sometimes both are called oral sex)
- Sexual contact with the rectum (touching or putting fingers, penis, tongue, or other things inside the opening in a child's bottom, called the anus)
- Putting fingers, penis, tongue, or objects inside the opening in a girl's vagina (also called vaginal penetration)
- Many other actions

People in *positions of authority* are adults: parents, grandparents, uncles or aunts, older brothers or sisters or cousins, babysitters, close friends of the family, teachers, coaches, scout leaders, ministers and priests, practically anyone you can think of whom children are taught to listen to, to obey, to

14

respect, to trust. Their jobs are to watch out for children and protect them from harm so that childhood can be full of wonderful growing experiences. Most people in these positions know how to use their authority correctly. Only the people who *require* sexual or other abusive activity from someone younger, less knowledgeable, or weaker than themselves abuse their positions of care and authority.

The group of people who are *smaller, younger,* or in other ways *less powerful* obviously includes younger children as victims of teenagers or adults. Sometimes people abuse someone who is almost the same age, exactly the same age, or even older than themselves. Children and adults with mental or physical disabilities can be abused by someone the same age or younger, for example.

Abusers have power in lots of different ways. Sometimes the abuser is bigger, more popular, more socially skilled, or smarter. Because the person who is abused is usually less powerful in the relationship, we say this person is *vulnerable* to (or at risk of) receiving abuse, through either *force* or *persuasion.* It is hard to say no to some abusers. A vulnerable child does not have an equal say in the decision to be sexually touched or to sexually touch someone else. Therefore, the person who is abused is called the *victim* of the abuser or simply an abused child or a child who was abused.

Force comes in many forms. Sometimes force means actual physical action in which someone is hit, pushed, or held. Sometimes the force is applied by using emotional or psychological coercion or persuasion, such as in threats of violence, severe punishment, or severe losses to the child or to others in the family.

Sometimes force comes in the form of bribes or special treats. The treats might be objects, such as toys or clothes, or ice cream or candy.

The treats might be promises of special privileges, such as staying up late or going someplace special. Or the treat might be the promise of special love from the abuser. The force or persuasion might even come in such a hidden way that the child does not feel forced. Often a child simply has no particular reason to say no or not to trust the person who asks for sexual activity. Abusers often know how to use techniques of persuasion to convince and to trick vulnerable children into thinking that they are part of the abusive activity.

Secret is different from *private*. Adults may choose to have sex in their own bedroom, and that is private. For a variety of reasons, children or adults at times may touch their own genitals while alone in their own bedrooms or bathrooms. These activities are private and are okay. Some secrets can be fun secrets, like a gift you made for someone or a surprise trip to the circus. These fun secrets are ones that make people feel good as soon as the secret happens and everyone finds out.[1]

Secrets about touching during sexual abuse are not fun secrets. They are unhappy secrets that abusers force on children. Unhappy secrets about touching make children feel confused and unsure about how they think or feel. Sometimes children like the secret touching because it feels good to have so much attention and physical affection; later on these same children often feel terrible about the secret touching and about themselves.

Remember all the fears about telling that children carry. They may be afraid that they will get into trouble or will be hurt if they tell. They may be afraid that someone else they care about will be hurt. Sometimes children are afraid that no one will love them anymore if they tell about the secret touching. Children are often afraid that their parents will be sad or angry or get divorced. Sometimes they are afraid that someone, either the abuser or the victim, will have to move out of their home.

Unhappy secrets about secret touching are ones that *make people feel bad inside* and scared that bad things will happen if anyone ever hears about the secret. The abuser often has taught the child to have these fears just so the child will not tell anyone about the secret touching. In *A Very Touching Book: For Little People and Big People*, Jan Hindman (1983) talks clearly about all the different kinds of touching and describes how secret touching hurts children. You may want to get this book from the library, borrow it from your therapist, or order it from a bookstore.

The term *sexual abuse* can be confusing. Sometimes abusive sexual touching hurts a lot and actually causes physical injury. Sometimes it does not seem to hurt at all, so it can be particularly confusing for children when we call it abuse. Sexual abuse of a child is about someone abusing a position of authority and power to violate the trust of a child. Sexual abuse is about hurting a child in hidden ways. It's important for children to understand that it is still abuse even when it doesn't physically hurt. Perhaps the words in the next few paragraphs will be useful when talking with your child.

You might explain to a child that sometimes sexual abuse doesn't hurt because the abuser is gentle and acts like he or she loves the child. Sometimes it doesn't hurt because our bodies are made so that skin feels good to touch and be touched. Otherwise, no one would ever hug or kiss or shake hands or play. Think about it. We couldn't do any activity at all if it hurt our skin to be touched. Rubbing skin can be a way of giving or receiving comfort, like when we rub our head when we have a headache, or we rub our muscles when they hurt. It's natural for our skin to give us good feelings.

Perhaps you can help your child understand the physical sensations experienced during the abuse. Children need to understand that it's natural that gentle touching of the genitals (privates) can feel good. That's partly the way genitals are made to be. The whole human race would not exist if touching genitals or having sex to make babies was painful. Genitals are parts of our bodies that are made to bring a special pleasure. Because those private parts are so special, no one has the right to force anyone else to share them. It's a big decision who to share them with, and a decision that should wait until a child is grown-up.[2] It is *never* okay for an adult to share sexual parts or activities with a child. Sometimes parents or other adults caring for children do touch private parts, like when they're changing the baby's diaper. That's okay. There's nothing secret about that kind of touching.

Sometimes kids get confused because during sexual abuse their skin might give them feelings of pleasure. This feeling of pleasure might make them think that they want the sexual activity to occur. What kids want, though, is pleasure and affection and attention—not sexual activity. While it is happening, some kids do not even think of it as abuse. Sometimes the abuser teaches kids to think of the sexual activity as a way to have a special loving relationship. Kids can become confused about what the abuser is telling them, about how their bodies are responding, and about their mixed feelings of shame and secrecy.

17

Sexual abuse is called *abuse* because it hurts people, sometimes on the outside of their bodies, but almost always on the inside of their minds and in their hearts. Sexual abuse in the family, called *incest*, can sometimes cause more harm than any other kind of abuse. Families are supposed to be safe places for children to grow up with adults who care for them and protect them from the harms of the world. Sexual abuse by a family member or even a trusted friend often hurts children more than sexual abuse by a stranger. Sexual abuse hurts because it mixes up the way the family members act toward and feel about each other. Sexual abuse hurts in families because the big secret about sexual touching sits like a big, dark cloud that no one wants to talk about.

In the pages that follow, we will be looking at all these issues as we attempt to lift the dark cloud, filled with the many thoughts and feelings your family might be experiencing.

Notes

1. Hindman, J. (1983). *A very touching book: For little people and big people.* Durkee, Ore.: AlexAndria Associates.

2. Hindman, J. (1983). *A very touching book: For little people and big people.* Durkee, Ore.: AlexAndria Associates.

2

....

Abuser or Victim: "That's Not All I Am!"

Sometimes people feel upset if others call them an abuser or a victim. "That's not all I am!" they say. Of course, no one should be thought of as *just* an abuser or *just* a victim or an abused child. No one is *just* a nonabusing parent or caretaker. Therapists and social workers use these terms to help everyone keep clear which person they are talking about and what that person's role is in the abuse situation, but they know that each person is much more than the label. It is helpful to think about all the other roles each person plays in life to get a clear picture of the whole person. Let's look at some examples.

Let's think about an uncle who is sexually abusing his niece. We call him an *abuser*. There are other things he might do during the week that could tell us more about who he is.

- Works hard at a steady job
- Is caring and loving at times
- Helps with school projects
- Plays with the kids
- Is active in church
- Can be thoughtful of others at times
- Helps his elderly mother
- Fixes things around the house
- Coaches soccer
- Is a good bowler

Sometimes a family might see just the part of the uncle who is caring and loving. And they miss seeing the part of the uncle that abuses. Using a circle graph, we can describe and picture all the parts that make up this uncle.

What if the abuser is a teenage girl who is sexually abusing her younger brother? Surely she participates in other activities that tell us who she is besides an abuser.

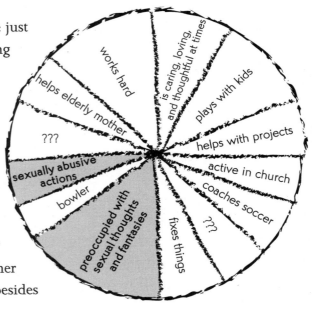

- Works at a part-time job after school
- Is thoughtful, loving, and caring at times
- . . . or may act mean or be a bully at times
- Drives her grandmother on errands
- Plays in the school band
- Likes basketball and swimming
- Volunteers in the soup kitchen

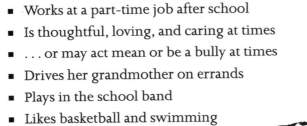

Often family members see, or want to see, just the girl who plays basketball, but they miss seeing the abusive behavior that the child does. Again, let's look at a circle graph.

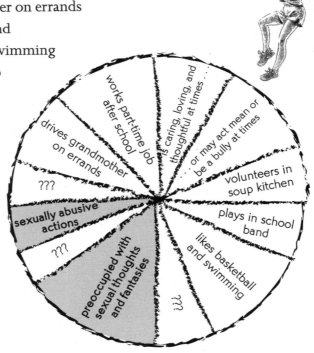

Now let's think about a child who is being sexually abused. Other than having been victimized, such a child might do lots of things that tell us who he or she is.

- Is caring and loving
- Helps out at home
- Goes biking with a sister or brother
- Works hard in school
- Plays on the soccer team
- Enjoys video and computer games
- Makes friends easily
- Helps her or his grandfather
- Plays with and takes care of his or her dog
- Has a great sense of humor
- Is active in Scouts
- Can set up a Web page

When parents and other family members see all these wonderful things about a child, they understandably have a hard time believing that the child could also be a victim of sexual abuse.

Children react to abuse in many ways. Some cover it up and look just fine on the outside, like the child above, while others cover it up with acting out and aggressive behavior. They might do lots of things that are upsetting.

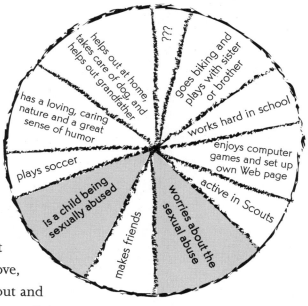

- Wet the bed
- Tell lies about some things, like doing chores or homework
- Fight physically with brothers or sisters
- Have trouble getting along with kids at school

- Throw temper tantrums
- Act or speak disrespectfully to parents or teachers
- Disobey or break rules
- Have difficulty paying attention or getting good grades in school

When children act out their unhappiness toward others and have trouble managing their behavior, sometimes it's hard to see the part inside them that has been hurt by sexual abuse. Again the circle graph can help us see how an abused child might look inside.

And now, let's consider the non-abusing parent, who could be a biological or adoptive parent, a foster parent, or any relative or adult guardian taking care of an abused child and/or a child who did the abusing. When sexual abuse occurs in a family, nonabusing parents react in many different ways. Sometimes, nonabusing parents are in total shock, particularly when the abuser has been extremely clever in keeping the abuse out of the nonabusing parent's awareness. At other times, nonabusing parents feel so saddened or angered or troubled by the abuse that they pay attention only to how bad they feel about not seeing or stopping the abuse. Sometimes after disclosure, nonabusing parents feel judged by others and by themselves. It can feel like all anyone sees is that they are parents of an abused or abusing child. While having these feelings is understandable, it is important to remember the positive qualities and strengths and the roles of the nonabusing parent that tell us who he or she is.

- Works to help support the family
- Attends parent-teacher conferences

- Volunteers in the local nursing home
- Loves and cares for the children
- Plans wonderful picnics and hikes
- Teaches each child how to ride a bike

And again, the circle graph helps to picture the many parts of the nonabusing parent.

In all abuse situations it is important to look at what was going on in the family that *might* have put the child at risk for abuse. This is not to say that the nonabusing parent is to blame for the abuse. The abuser is responsible for the sexual abuse of a child. But it is important for nonabusing parents to think back and see if anything could or should have been done earlier to protect the child and, if so, to take responsibility for not doing it. For example, some nonabusing parents might have sensed that something was wrong, but rather than react protectively, they blocked out any awareness by abusing alcohol or drugs. Some problem areas that might contribute to a situation where abuse could occur are:

- Being afraid of the abuser
- Being so afraid of life without the abuser that the fear reduced awareness or fostered denial or minimization of what was going on
- Having low self-esteem and a lack of self-confidence
- Abusing alcohol or drugs to lower anxiety, to alleviate depression, or to dull the senses
- Having a conflict-ridden relationship with the child
- Being away from home an excessive amount of time, more than is necessary
- Being involved in unhealthy or abusive adult relationships

Like most people, nonabusing parents can have a mixture of strengths and problem areas. The following circle graph helps to picture the many parts of the nonabusing parent who also has some personal problem areas.

All members of the family have lots of parts to their personalities. It is all these other parts that make people interesting and lovable. But we can't ignore the part of the person that is being affected by sexual abuse. Even while the person is involved in those other activities, the sexual abuse is often still on his or her mind.

- How much time do you think sexual abuse actually takes? Does it take just a few minutes a day? A week?
- Does the abuser think about it during the day, even while working?
- Does the child worry about the sexual touching while sleeping at night, trying to concentrate on work at school, or playing soccer?
- Does the sexual abuse ever go out of the child's mind? For how long?
- Does the sexual abuse ever go out of the abuser's mind? For how long?

Here's a way to think about it. Divide the blank circles on the next page to show how each person in your family looks to you, like the pie charts you've already seen. Be sure to show what part of the person has been affected by the abuse or abusive behavior. How much does it affect the person while the abuse is occurring? How much time does each person think about, plan, or worry about the abuse?

24

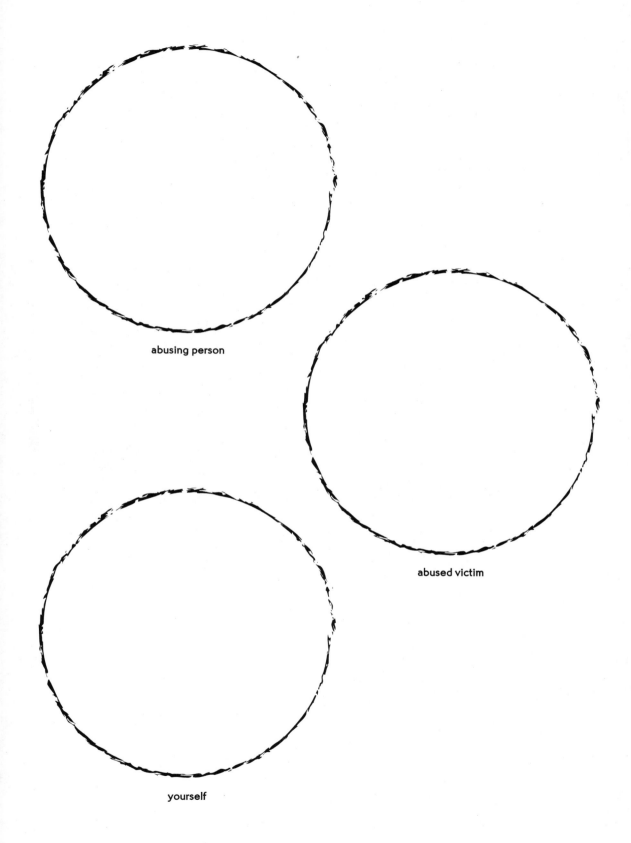

abusing person

abused victim

yourself

It is really clear that every person is made up of lots of wonderful parts — interests, jobs, activities, and personalities. The part of a person that sexual abuse affects, the part that has been victimized, however, is the part that may need repair. The part of a person that abuses, the offending part, is the part that needs correction and change. And any part of a person that reduces child safety in the family, the diminished-ability-to-protect part, is the part that needs to change. It is important to face the problem of sexual abuse in the same responsible way you would face other problems. When you ignore problems inside yourself, sometimes those problems can become bigger and bigger. You can probably think of lots of times in other parts of your life when that could be true. Imagine, for example, you have a cavity in a tooth. That does not mean the rest of your teeth are no good. It does mean that you must go to a dentist. If you do not get the decay taken care of, it can spread and ruin the whole tooth, or other nearby teeth. It can even cause infection that can spread further in the mouth and even further into the body.

Just like this cavity needs to be treated by an expert, a dentist, sexual abuse is a problem that counseling can help correct to keep it from ruining the health of a child and of a whole family. This example — of sexual abuse being like a cavity — is a "metaphor": a story that uses something we do understand, like how tooth decay can spread, to learn about something we don't understand, like how sexual touching problems can spread. Metaphors are parallel situations or stories that help us understand something complicated by looking at something that is similar but maybe not so complicated.

section II: understanding the sexual abuser

3

....

Finding Out What the Abuser Did

It is understandable that at first abusers tell only part of what they've done. They are not proud of their behavior. They may be embarrassed or ashamed. They are worried about how angry people will be with them, and they definitely do not want to get into any more trouble than they are already in. Or, they may be in a condition called *denial* — when they deny not only to others, but also to themselves, that they have abused someone. It is too mentally painful and emotionally shameful for them to admit how they have taken advantage of a child and hurt their whole family.

Sometimes, abusers admit part of the abuse, but they *minimize* how much they did or how much the abuse might have hurt the child. Minimizing is making something seem like less than it is — less important, less painful, less frequent.

So, the information we hear about the sexual abuse in the beginning is usually just a small part of the truth, just the "tip of the iceberg." There is usually more information about the sexually abusive behavior

27

that the abuser keeps hidden as long as possible. If treatment is going to be successful, it is important for the abuser to be totally honest about his or her history of sexually abusive behavior.

Truth Is Like an Onion

For abusers, getting to the whole truth may take a while. You may hear several stories about what happened. But there are certain facts about the abuse that together give a picture of the truth.

It takes a lot of courage to deal with the truth. Sometimes the facts come out a little bit at a time. Just when we think we know the whole truth, we find out there are more facts hidden underneath. Getting at the truth is like peeling an onion: you can take off layer after layer after layer before you get to the core.

With children, getting to the whole truth is not easy. Children usually are afraid to tell *anything* about the abuse, never mind tell *everything*! Remember, children understandably keep silent about their own sexual abuse for many reasons, but mostly because they are afraid of losing love, people, or safety or making people angry or upset. When their unhappiness becomes too overwhelming to manage, children sometimes begin to tell just a little bit about their abuse experience to a friend, a teacher, or someone else they trust. Telling about the sexual abuse is called a *disclosure* or an *allegation*. People's responses to this information—even when the responses are good, positive, and supportive—can be even more overwhelming and frightening to children. A friend might tell a parent or a counselor, who then reports the information to a protective agency to investigate.

When other family members—even the adults—are also too scared about what might happen, there is no family support for the child to tell the whole truth about the abuse. Abused children in these families might feel that the family is in emotional pain from feeling scared, exposed, ashamed, or invaded, and it is *their* fault. They may wish that they had never said anything to anyone. In fact, sometimes the things that an abuser threatened would happen actually come true: someone moves out of the home, someone is arrested, someone goes to jail, some people become angry at the whole situation, and some people become angry at the victim for telling.

Sometimes children who disclose sexual abuse feel that no one in the family believes them. Sometimes they feel like no one loves them anymore. Children in these situations may think that if they could take back everything they said, the family would be happy again. These children do not want to be abused anymore, but they do not want to live with so much anger either. That's why frightened children sometimes take everything back and say the abuse never happened. This process of "taking back" the information, of saying that the sexual abuse never happened, is called retracting[1] or recanting.[2]

When children recant or take back their statements about sexual abuse that really did happen, they do it to protect themselves, the abuser, and their family. Unfortunately, children who recant about real sexual abuse may be at even higher risk of being abused again. After all, if no one believed them the first time they told, why would they tell again? By giving up on telling the truth about their abuse, these children may give up their chance at having the strength to tell and to protect themselves from abuse in the future. A child who recants may be labeled a liar, even though he or she did tell the truth about the abuse at first. Recanting usually means the child is scared and upset and needs more support than ever.

For a while after disclosure, it may seem like facts about what happened are hard to come by. The story may seem slippery, changing a little each time it is told. Sometimes children test parents' or friends' reactions by telling just a little bit to see whether it is safe before telling more. Abusers may tell as little as they can get away with. But progress toward healing from abuse means that eventually everyone must tell the whole truth and face all the facts.

Notes

1. Summit, R.C. (1983). The child abuse accommodation syndrome. Child Abuse and Neglect, 7, 177–193.

2. Berliner, L., & Elliot, D. M. (1996). Sexual abuse of children. In J. Briere, L. Berliner, J. A. Bulkley, C. Jenny, & T. Reid (Eds.), *The APSAC handbook on child maltreatment* (pp. 51–71). Thousand Oaks, Calif.: Sage.

4

It's a Puzzle: Why Do Abusers Do It?

One of the first and most troubling tasks families often take on is looking for an explanation for why the abuser did it. "Why" is a natural focus for families, but there is no single, clear answer to that question. Usually, the focus of the abuser's treatment will be on understanding and explaining the "who, what, when, where, and how" of what he or she did, and on interrupting that pattern. Understanding some of the things that lead up to abusive behavior, however, can be helpful.

Sometimes abusers feel bad and worthless. Making a child do sexual things with them helps them feel a little better for a little while. Sometimes they don't feel very sure about their ability to have close relationships with people their own age. Making a child do sexual things with them helps them feel cared about. Sometimes they want total control in a relationship. Sometimes they are excited by sexual behavior that is forbidden in their culture or by their religion. Sexual abusers choose children because children are available (easy to get to) and *controllable*. These are just some of the possible reasons that someone would sexually abuse a child.

Abusers use lots of excuses and partial explanations. Abusive adults may say they did it because they were drinking or were depressed. They may say they did it because someone abused them in childhood. They may say it was an accident or that the child started it. Abusive older children may say they did it as an experiment, to learn about sex. Those statements may be partly true, but they are not the whole truth. There are lots of people who drink but never sexually abuse a child. There are lots of kids who are curious about sex but don't learn about it with someone smaller than them in their own family. They wait and learn about sexual activity with someone their own age whom they do not have to trick or bribe or force into sexual activity.

While you may hear an abuser offer many excuses, basically there is one answer to "why?": the abuser *made a choice* to sexually abuse a child. Still, it is important for the abuser to figure out all the pieces of that decision to abuse. Perhaps a useful way to understand this problem behavior is to think of it as a puzzle. It may be a 10-piece puzzle, or a 50-piece puzzle. Abusers must act like detectives, looking for all the clues about why and how they chose to abuse someone.

Therapists can help abusers discover the clues by talking with them about their lives and about the way they think. Abusers can keep track of those clues and learn what they can change and what they can't. One of the easiest ways for abusers to keep track of their own clues is to make up a puzzle and put the clue-pieces together. If you are an abuser and can identify all the pieces, you will have the whole picture about your behavior. Once abusers fully understand their behavior, they can begin to work really hard in treatment to change some pieces of the puzzle. If they can change enough pieces, they can learn how to keep themselves from ever abusing a child again. In the puzzle shown here, think about which pieces (clues) an abuser could change and which pieces could become excuses for continuing sexually abusive behavior.

Learning to change any behavior is difficult. You have seen people trying to change other behaviors or habits, such as drinking or smoking or biting their fingernails. Sometimes it takes a long time before they actually change, even though they've promised others, and even themselves, that they can do it. Do you know anyone who ever tried to give up smoking? Or drinking? Or stay on a diet? Or commit to daily exercise to get in shape?

People often *want* to change their habits but just do not seem to be able to do it the first time they try. Sometimes they have to try again and again before they really can make a change last. Or sometimes they can change one thing, like smoking, but can't stick to their promise to stop gambling. If sexual abusers really want to change their behavior, they must be honest and tell everyone about their tricks (*thinking errors, manipulations*). They must work hard to learn new ways to think and new ways to control their own behavior. Their new knowledge and skills can help them stick to their promise never to abuse again. And finally, they must not use their behavior problem to keep controlling the family. To change, the abuser must be willing to give up control over others and to work on gaining control over himself or herself.

Thinking Errors: Reasons or Excuses?

Here's a list of some things abusers might say about their behavior:

- "It was an accident — my hand just fell there while I was watching TV."
- "I was only trying to show affection and feel close to her."
- "I was only teaching him about his body and sex."
- "It only happened because I was drinking."
- "It was only because my wife and I weren't getting along and weren't having sex."
- "She misunderstood . . . I'll talk with her."
- "We were just wrestling . . . all families do it!"
- "But he likes to be tickled . . . I'll be more careful next time."
- "I was just jealous and angry. My parents give her all their attention."
- "It wasn't all my fault. She liked it. Besides, lots of times she came to me first."
- "It's her fault — just look at the way she dresses — she's asking for it."
- "He's only a child. He always lies about lots of things."
- "What are you accusing me of? You must have a sick mind to think like that!"

You may have heard statements like these for so long that at first they sound true. But do the thoughts underneath these statements sound like reasons or excuses? Is the abuser taking responsibility for his or her actions, or trying to blame the child, the spouse, or the parents? Is the abuser accepting criticism, or using anger to get someone to back off from the sense that something is wrong? These are examples of how abusers mix up their thinking — and try to mix up yours — to get what they want.

People who can sexually abuse a child think differently about children and about themselves than do other people who would never consider sexually abusing a child. This can be confusing, because at times abusers *seem* to be the kind of people who are loving and caring with children. It's true that in some situations abusers can be caring about others. But people who act in truly caring and loving ways think *first* about others, not about themselves. People who think about what is best for children before thinking of their own needs do not use and hurt children or hurt their whole family. Let's look at how the abuser in your family came to think that it was okay to sexually abuse a child.

In order to abuse a child, sexual abusers stop thinking about what is best for the child and the family. They change (distort) the way they are thinking, so they will not feel so bad about what they are doing or about themselves. We call these mistakes in thinking *excuses* or *thinking errors* or *cognitive distortions*.[1] Sexual abusers use this mixed-up thinking to *trick* or *manipulate* their victims and other members of the families. *Thinking errors* are thoughts twisted around the truth, in order to avoid responsibility or to change or distort the truth.

Abusers know their behavior is wrong, so they use thinking errors to allow themselves (and possibly their victims) to think that touching a child sexually is okay. Let's look again at the first statement on our list: "It was an accident — my hand just fell there while I was watching TV." Realistically, it's pretty hard to touch someone's genitals by accident. Most of the time, genitals are protected between the legs, and it's pretty easy to figure out if someone has touched your genitals or your breasts without your permission. You just feel it and know it.

33

Another statement on the list puts blame on the abuser's wife because of problems in their sexual relationship. Many people have sexual difficulties, but they do not reach out for a child as a substitute for an adult partner. Now let's take a longer look at some of the other statements or excuses abusers use. If you listen carefully, you can hear the excuses or thinking errors in each of them.

"It Just Happened One Time!"

Often an abuser tells everyone, "It just happened. I didn't plan it. Honest, it only happened one time. It will *never* happen again!" The language the abuser uses shows that he or she is avoiding responsibility. First of all, "it happened" is the correct phrase only in situations over which no *person* has control: "The river flooded . . . *it happened* in May." "The tree branch fell into the yard . . . *it happened* during the storm."

But it does not make sense to use "it happened" in this situation: "The baseball went into Mrs. Brown's window . . . it happened while practicing in the yard." Who is responsible for "*it*"?

We should say, "*Frankie* hit the baseball through Mrs. Brown's window. *He* did it during the game." Now we know that Frankie is the one responsible, and we can expect him to take

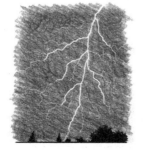

responsibility by admitting what he did and paying for a new window.

Second, because the phrase "it just happened" tells us that no one has control over the situation, that same phrase tells us that "it" could "happen" again, and there's nothing we can do to stop it. The situation is out of our control. Events in nature are like that. A bolt of lightning *happens* in a split second. Even if we see lightning strike one place, we have no way to tell where it might strike the next time.

When abusers say the sexual abuse "just happened," they are declaring that they are out of control. They are comparing their behavior to the unpredictability of a bolt of lightning.

Unless the abuser changes, it is doubtful that treatment can help him or her. It would be like trying to teach lightning how to stop flashing.

We know that most abusers learned their behavior as a way of meeting some emotional need. We also know that many abusers can learn other ways to meet their needs that don't hurt anyone.

It is true that some abusers are not treatable because they cannot give up their desire to use children sexually. But many other abusers *can* learn to control their behavior. The first step is for them to take responsibility for what they have done and for the choices they have made.

Sometimes it is true when an abuser says, "It only happened once. It's never happened before in my whole life." Sometimes the abuse stops after the first time because the child was able to tell someone who could help. Or perhaps another adult in the home discovered the abuse right away and took action to protect the child. Much of the time, however, sexual abuse goes on for a long time before it is reported or discovered.

"It Wasn't All My Fault! She Came to Me First"

Can you figure out the *thinking error* in this statement? "She enjoyed it. She came to me first. It's not my fault." Most sexual abusers are aware of their own feelings and what *they* want but don't really stop to think or care about how their victims are feeling during the abuse. Abusers let themselves believe what they want to believe. Abuse can feel terrible, confusing, or even sort of okay for part of it.

As you read earlier, the touching of skin and genitals during abuse might create feelings of pleasure in the child — it's a natural reaction that is built in to our bodies. This experience can be so confusing that it's worth spending more time with it here, especially if it helps you talk about this with your children.

Just think, if gentle touching or stroking of the skin did not feel good, we would never give hugs. It would hurt too much. Our skin is made so that it feels good when it is touched gently or firmly all over our bodies, including the genitals. There's nothing we can do about it. That's how skin is.

Right now, gently rub an area on your hand or your arm. It feels nice and comforting somehow, doesn't it? When we're sad or upset, one way our relatives and friends may try to help us feel better is by giving hugs or by holding or patting our hands. Our skin also lets us know when we are hurt, like when someone slaps us or kicks us. Our skin stings, turns red, maybe even bruises and swells up. There's nothing we can do about our body's reaction.

But even if a child likes the feeling of his or her skin and genitals being touched gently, that does not mean he or she liked all the other unhappy feelings that might have been going on at the same time. How the child feels about the sexual activity while it is occurring should not determine whether or not the activity occurs. Protective adults do not make decisions for children based simply on whether a child likes or wants something. Sure, some decisions can be based on whether kids like things. Kids should get to choose whether they like cookie dough ice cream or plain vanilla, whether they want to go to the circus or a movie, or whether they prefer riding a bicycle or rollerblading. These are all fun things that are good for kids.

But what if kids want to do something that's not good for them? Would protecting adults let them do it anyway? Family members are responsible for watching out for younger kids, so that they don't get hurt or in trouble. Adults would not be doing their job if they just let kids do whatever they wanted. For example, if Jeremiah wants to stay up every day until midnight, should his parents allow it? If Caitlin wants a bowl of candy for breakfast, should her grandparents let her eat it? If Keshawn wants to drink some alcohol, should his babysitter let him? Or if Janeen wants to drive the car down the street, should her stepfather allow it?

Just imagine this scene: Janeen, who is seven, says to her stepfather, "I want to drive the car down the street. Please, please can I? I know I can do it. I can reach the pedals. I know how to steer. I remember everything you taught me practicing in the driveway. Please! I just love it and I really want to!"

With that, she takes her stepfather's hand and pulls him to the car. What should Janeen's stepfather do? Should he just smile, and say "Okay"? Try to picture how a police officer who stopped the car would react to the stepfather's explanation, "It's not my fault, officer. She really wanted to. She likes it."

It's the responsibility of adults and older adolescents to set an example that teaches young children right from wrong and to set limits around what children are allowed to do according to their age and abilities. It's every parent's job to keep children safe from sexual abuse so that they can learn about and experience sex at the right age, with people their own age, when they are able to make their own choice to do so.

"He's Always Been a Bad Seed. My Sexually Abusing Him Didn't Cause His Problems"

Sometimes abusers try to minimize the amount of harm (make it seem less) or even deny that they have done any harm to a child. They try to blame someone else, even the child. Some abusers use the excuse that the child has always been a problem, has been messed up for years, long before the abuser did anything. These abusers suggest that the sexual abuse was not that bad compared with the harm other people caused in the child's life. By using this excuse, abusers are saying that they should not be held responsible or accountable for the sexual abuse, "since it didn't really cause any great harm." Let's look at a real-life example in which we use made-up names.

Jason's father deserted the family; his mother was an alcoholic who had been beating him for years. The local child protective agency investigated and eventually removed him from his home and brought him to live with an aunt and uncle. Jason later disclosed that his aunt was sexually abusing him. She admitted to the abuse but took no responsibility for adding to the boy's problems, saying, "That kid was messed up long before I even touched him. He has never done well in school. He started shoplifting when he was nine. He's in trouble all the time. He's just a 'bad seed.'"

Yes, Jason's behavior at the time he came to live with his aunt's family probably had a lot to do with those earlier years of physical abuse and neglect. But as a parent figure, Jason's aunt had the responsibility of giving him a new family experience that could help correct the negative ways he had learned. She could have taught him that adults *could* be trustworthy and caring, that adults *could* be counted on for guidance, that adults were *not* always abusive and neglectful. His aunt's job was to act like a good parent, make a positive difference in Jason's life, and give him a safe place where he could grow up. She didn't do that.

What about this idea of "bad seed"? This old, country expression suggests that if a plant does not grow well, it is not the farmer's fault. It's just that he had a bad seed.

When abusers think of a child as "bad seed," they are using a thinking error to change the truth. If they can trick themselves into thinking of the child as no good, then abusers do not have to feel so bad about sexually abusing the child. After all, it's pretty hard to worry about damaging something that is already regarded as "worthless," ready to be thrown out with the trash.

Think for a minute, however, about how people decide whether something *is* junk. Sometimes things that one person tosses out as junk are worth saving to another person. The "junk" might need only a new coat of paint or a broken piece glued together to become a "real find," a "treasure." And sometimes "messed up," hurt kids need just one good friend, some love, and help in healing to become treasures.

In fact, the whole "bad seed" concept needs closer examination. Sometimes when a plant isn't growing well, it isn't because the seed is bad—it's because the seed hasn't received good care. Maybe it didn't get enough water, or it got too much manure and not enough bone meal, or slugs and bugs got to it. Perhaps someone stepped on it. Maybe there were conditions beyond the farmer's control, such as an ice storm or not enough rain. The plant just couldn't thrive — until, that is, someone transplanted it to a more protected area and gave it the right kind of attention.

Thinking of people as "bad seeds" or worthless trash is not realistic or useful. It makes more sense to think of people as having problems and behaviors that they can change. If children develop problems early in life, they need to be with adults who can give them the right kind of attention and help them overcome their problems so that they can grow healthy and strong.

Note

1. Abel, G. G., Gore, D. K., Holland, C. L., Camp, N., Becker, J. V., & Rathner, J. (1989). The measurement of the cognitive distortions of child molesters. *Annals of Sex Research, 2,* 135–152.

Faller, K. C. (1993). *Child sexual abuse: Intervention and treatment issues.* Manual of U.S. Department of Health and Human Services, Administration for Children and Families. McLean, Va.: The Circle.

Murphy, W. D. (1990). Assessment and modification of cognitive distortions in sex offenders. In W. L. Marshall, D. R. Laws, & H. E. Barbaree (Eds.), *Handbook of sexual assault: Issues, theories, and treatment of the offender* (pp. 331–342). New York: Plenum.

5

....

Sexual Abuse Is a Hard-to-Stop, Complicated Problem

Remember when we said there are many reasons why someone sexually abuses a child? The abuser's job in treatment is to figure out how this problem behavior developed and to learn how to *not* do it again. Children do not cause their own sexual abuse. People who sexually abuse children have stopped fully caring about the child and mostly care about their secret sexual behavior. Sometimes sexual abusers really do feel bad about their behavior, but still they don't stop. They don't stop because they get feelings of importance, of power, of control from doing the sexual abuse. They may even imagine they are being loved by and are being loving to the child. But in a real loving relationship, each person wants what is best for the other. Sexual abusers often trick children into thinking that loving the abuser through sexual behavior is good, a special part of their relationship, but the abuser knows all along that this sexual behavior is not good for the child. Sexual abusers are stuck in thinking about what they want for themselves.

If abusers really thought what they were doing was okay, they would be telling everyone about the sexual touching. When people feel good about what they are doing, they are not afraid someone will find out. Think of all the times we hear people talk proudly about what they are doing. "Hey, I'm teaching my younger brother how to play baseball. We're having a lot of fun together," or " I'm teaching my daughter how to play chess."

Each abuser's behavior "puzzle" has different pieces, and some of those pieces are about why they don't stop. Many abusers report feeling bad about themselves even while they are abusing a child. A few abusers are able to stop and report themselves, but most abusers continue abusing even though they know it is wrong and harmful. There are lots of different reasons for each individual abuser's behavior. There is one reason, however, that they all share for not stopping their offending. Sexual abusers do not stop because the good feelings they get from their sexually abusing behavior are stronger or more important to them than the bad feelings they get from knowing they are doing something that hurts someone else. Abusers often do not stop because they have changed (distorted) their way of thinking in order to feel okay about themselves and continue abusing. The good feelings they get from the sexually abusive behavior make them want to have more of these good feelings, so over time they think less and less about the bad feelings.

Sexual abuse does not occur by accident or without warning. Sexually abusive behavior usually develops over time, in stages. The stages might have developed over a few months, or over many years. The stages might have begun in childhood, or not until adulthood. The stages and ages they began are different for each abuser. But over time, for each sexual abuser there is a gradually increasing amount of time he or she spends thinking sexual thoughts and acting out in sexual ways. There is a gradually increasing amount of time he or she spends distorting his or her thinking to block out awareness of how the abuse is hurting the child and the family.

For abusers to change, it is not enough just to be aware of these sexual thoughts and these distortions in thinking. If abusers want to change, they need to develop and choose other ways of making themselves feel better that don't hurt anyone. Let's look at some of the reasons that abusers hang on to their abusive thoughts.

Thinking Ahead and Planning to Abuse

Sometimes we hear abusers deny that they have a problem. They say that this child is the only one they have ever touched, and therefore it is something about the *child*, not about them. Abusers may say this because they have a hard time admitting to themselves or to others that they have abused other children. Abusers often have more than one victim, but sometimes there are no other victims.

But before abusers actually do any abusing, whether it is one child or many, they start *thinking* about sexual touching. They use a lot of *thinking errors*. Then they usually start *planning* how they can set up a situation so they can touch the child. This process is no different from planning any crime. Think of a robbery, for example. The robber doesn't just walk down the street one day and suddenly drop into a bank to steal the money. Usually the robber has been thinking for a long time about how much money he or she wants and how to get it.

This robber might think that life is unfair. He or she might feel self-pity or be angry at others who seem to have more money and possessions. The person might start thinking about the easiest place to rob. Then she or he might go into a local gas station or convenience store, pretending to be a customer, just to check out where the cash register is or what shifts have only one employee working. Then the robber starts using *thinking errors* a lot: "Hey, it's no big deal this one time. The insurance company will pay for it, so it's not like the store owner will really lose out. There is no way I can stretch my paycheck to buy everything I need; they keep us poor on purpose. Hey, rich people steal too — they just do it through cheating on taxes. It's the little guy that never gets a break."

Long before the theft, the robber has already begun twisting his or her thinking so that it seems okay to steal. If the robber is successful at stealing from little places, then he or she becomes more confident and turns to stealing from bigger stores or banks. Or the robber increases the risk by breaking into people's homes. Many movies show robbers carefully planning their crimes weeks in advance. The first time the robber gets caught stealing, he or she might say, "Hey, I'm not really a thief. I just did it this one time."

The robber knows, however, that he or she *has* stolen before — it's just that the robber has never been caught before. Maybe the first theft was from a sister or brother when the robber was young. Next was taking money from his or her father's wallet, or from someone's locker in school. Even stealing someone else's answers — cheating on a test — is a kind of theft. The robber might have a lifetime pattern of being dishonest and can't stop thinking about how to take things that don't belong to him or her.

When it comes to sexual abuse, abusers usually think like robbers and other criminals. Sexual abusers also steal from people, even though family members may not realize all the things the abuser has stolen from them. You can read more about how sexual abusers rob their victims and their families in Part Two, "How Much Harm?"

Like the robber who said that it was his first bank, the abuser may be accurate in saying that this is his or her first abuse victim. Just as we can trace a robber's behavior to discover the thinking before the crime, we can trace an abuser's behavior to discover the thinking before the touching.

Almost everyone thinks about sex sometimes. That is perfectly normal. Sexual abusers, however, are *preoccupied* with thinking about sex and specifically about sexually abusive behavior. They think about this behavior so much that they let their abusive thoughts control their behavior.

Abusers *can* learn to control or change their thoughts and their abusive sexual behavior. First, they have to become aware of the series of "seemingly unimportant decisions" they make all along the way toward actually beginning the abusive behavior.[1] When a person with an alcohol problem is trying to change, one thing the person must do is look at all the small ways that alcohol comes into his or her life, from buying beer on the way home from work and keeping booze in a cupboard, to having a few beers in front of the TV, to always meeting friends in a bar. In the same way, abusers must analyze the small steps that have become part of the habitual behavior they repeat over and over in a cycle of choices. When they are able to understand this cycle, they are better able to make different choices away from the path of sexual abuse. Once abusers are able to make different choices, they have the knowledge of how to bring their behavior under control.

We know that no one is born a sexual abuser or becomes a sexual abuser all at once. Somewhere along the way, from birth to when the abuse was disclosed, he or she learned to use sexually abusive thinking and behavior as a solution to some problem or need. The abuser probably has had some form of sexual preoccupation problem for a long time. One way to trace the abuser's history of thoughts and behavior is to use a *time line* to track his or her sexual history. A time line is simply a line used to plot out events or behaviors over a period of time.

Following is a made-up example of a time line that traces the growth of sexually abusive behavior from childhood and connects it to other events or important times in the abuser's life. For example, we can see that this man was unhappy at age 11, about the time he was sexually abused by a teenage friend. Then at age 13, still lonely and unhappy, he touched a 6-year-old boy, and at age 15, he began to use pornography. By age 19, he was *preoccupied* with sexual thoughts and the desire to masturbate and to use pornography.

One Abuser's Time Line

LIFE-EVENTS HISTORY	AGE	SEXUAL HISTORY
Lots of family fighting	10	Normal interest in masturbation begins
Unhappy and anxious	11	Sexually touched by older teenager
	12	
Lonely/acne, self-conscious	13	Touches a 6-year-old boy
	14	Masturbates a lot
Problems with peers	15	Uses pornography
	16	
	17	
Begins dating	18	Forces sex on girlfriend
Goes into the army	19	Uses prostitutes
	20	Preoccupied with masturbation
Discharged from the army	21	
Babysits for niece	22	Touches niece's genitals
Lonely, drinks a lot	23	Uses pornography/videos
	24	
	25	
Finds a girlfriend	26	Mutual peer-age consenting sex
Gets married	27	Sexual relationship with wife
Marital stress high, drinks a lot	28	Masturbates daily while watching videos
Daughter is born	29	Sex with wife is not satisfying
	30	
	31	Makes passes at women frequently
Drinks heavily, bored with life	32	Has a sexual relationship outside of marriage
	33	Begins thinking about touching daughter
Loses job; feels depressed	*34*	*Sexually touches daughter*
	35	Uses more videos and masturbates more often
Son is born	*36*	*Sexually touches daughter more frequently*
	37	*Sexual abuse progresses to more intense level*
Daughter discloses abuse	*38*	**Arrested for sexual abuse of daughter**

At age 22, he sexually abused his niece. He had a period of mutual sexual involvement with people near his own age before and during his marriage. But then he returned to his inappropriate sexual thoughts and fantasies, and eventually to sexually abusive behavior as he became bored and dissatisfied with his life. By connecting moods and life events to sexually acting-out behavior, this abuser could learn about his high-risk times for using sexual abuse of a child to feel better about himself.

Thinking About Sexual Abuse Is Different from Thinking About Sex

Abusers might *want* to stop thinking about sexually abusive behavior, but if they do not admit to themselves that they are doing something wrong, they are not ready to stop. If they have not been in specialized sexual abuse counseling, it is much harder for them to learn how to stop. There is a strong force inside their minds that keeps them thinking about sexual behavior and controlling others.

Thinking about sex is not wrong. It is a natural part of being a person. Just like hunger makes us think about food, or thirst makes us think about water, or tiredness makes us think about sleep, our sexual energies and feelings make us think about sex. A problem occurs only when a person thinks about sex too much of the time or in such a way that he or she takes advantage of someone who is more vulnerable. Most of us do not think about sex all the time; we are too busy with the rest of our lives. But our sexual energy is still there underneath the surface to use when we decide we want to be sexual. It is a little like having crude oil beneath the surface of the earth. The oil can sit there for months, even years, and never be used, but when we want or need the oil, we can just drill down to reach it.

When we have pumped out enough oil, we can put a cap on top of the oil well and save the oil until we want it again. People are in control of the oil; the oil is not in

45

control of people. We do not need to worry about the oil coming to the surface when we don't want it, because the earth is solid, acting like a strong  container to keep the oil in place. Imagine what it would be like if there was no strong, solid earth and rock to keep the oil beneath the surface.

The oil could spurt up through the earth into places where it shouldn't be, like in the middle of your driveway, or in your cellar, or even in the middle of your family room. No one would have control over the oil. Instead, the oil would be out of control, erupting to the surface wherever there was a weakness in the earth's floor.

This is how it is for people who think too much about sex. It is like this for sexual abusers who think about sexual contact with children. They do not have a good, solid "container" or "cap" to keep their sexual thoughts and behaviors under control. They think about sex so often that their thoughts get stronger and stronger and grow into a force beneath the surface. Sometimes their thoughts may come out in normal sexual behaviors, but most of the time, abusers' thoughts come out in unacceptable, harmful sexual behavior that includes sexual contact with children.

The Urge to Abuse Is Like a Train Without Brakes

Some abusers do not want to stop their behavior. Yet even when they do want to stop, they have a really hard time. They may find it particularly hard to stop if the abusive behavior has been going on for a long time. The longer the abuse goes on, the stronger a sexual abuser's focus on sex and sexually abusive behavior gets.

Have you ever watched how a train operates? When it first starts up, it goes slowly. The more fuel the engineer gives the engine, the faster it goes. Finally, the train builds to full speed. There is so much force pushing the train along that the brakes are often not strong enough to stop the train, even when the engineer sees something on the track. Can you imagine a train trying to stop if it had no brakes at all?

Sexual abusers often start slowly and in small ways with their inappropriate behavior. The more they do it and the more they get away with it, the stronger their thoughts grow. These thoughts become the fuel for their sexually abusive behaviors. They sometimes feel bad about their behavior and promise their victims or themselves that they will stop. These promise-thoughts, however, usually are not strong enough "brakes" to stop them, even when they know they are hurting a child. Their thoughts around stopping the abuse are much weaker than their thoughts around continuing. Often it is as if they have no brakes at all.

Is It About Power and Control, or About Sex?

Sexual abuse is about one person, the abuser, using power and control to victimize another smaller, less powerful person through sexual behavior. There are many reasons why abusers think they need to use a child to feel powerful and in control. Perhaps there are things in life that make them feel powerless—like losing a job, or having a serious medical or physical problem, or not having self-confidence, or having a lot of difficulty making friends, or getting poor grades in school, or not getting picked for a sports team. These things also happen to lots of other people, but they aren't coping with their frustrations or failures by *sexually abusing a child*. So, we have to go back and figure out the pieces of the puzzle before we have all the answers.

One piece of the puzzle we can't ignore is the piece about *sex*. Sometimes we hear that sexual abuse is about power and control and that it's not about sex. But there are many ways to gain power and control that have nothing to do with sex. People can be leaders at work or in school, organize their own clubs, or start their own businesses. When people use sexual activity to control someone else, this is sexual abuse, and it is partly about the abuser's pleasure in having sex this way.

Sometimes we hear that sexual abuse is an addiction or a compulsion. We say that people are *addicted* when they keep doing or using something that they know is wrong and is harmful to themselves and others. We say that people's behavior is *compulsive* when they continue to repeat behaviors over and over, even when they tell themselves they want to stop. People repeat addictive and compulsive behaviors sometimes to reduce anxiety, sometimes in an attempt to feel "normal," but almost always to give themselves temporary good feelings. They get so dependent on these ways of feeling good that they don't think of anything else. At the same time, these behaviors often cause people to feel ashamed, to imagine themselves as powerless and out of control.

But sexual abuse of children is not simply about sexual addictions or compulsions. There are many people who struggle with sexually addictive and other compulsive behaviors, but they do not cross the line and use children in sexual ways. Let's think about other addictive or compulsive behaviors to see what similarities and differences there might be between them and sexual abuse.

Think about cigarette smoking or drug or alcohol abuse. These habitual behaviors become *addictive* not only because of the person's emotional dependence on the behaviors but also because of the withdrawal symptoms from the chemical dependence on nicotine or other addictive substance. People have a hard time giving up these addictions even when they understand the health and social problems related to these behaviors.

Cigarette smoking is known to contribute to all kinds of lung problems and cancer. Alcohol or drug abuse can cause family problems, medical problems, driving problems, and overall general functioning problems. Yet people have a hard time stopping. They tell themselves, "Smoking helps me relax when I am under a lot of stress." "Drinking gives me something to do in social situations."

Think about *compulsive* habits some people develop, such as compulsive eating. Eating is part of normal, everyday life, but for some people, it becomes a compulsive habit. It may be that they overeat for emotional reasons—perhaps because they are lonely or depressed or overtired or

under a lot of stress. When they eat, they may get temporary relief from those emotionally painful feelings.

But their compulsive eating is also reinforced by the
early feelings of physical pleasure they get from the
foods they eat. People do not usually keep eating food
unless it *tastes* good. How many people do you
know who overeat brussels sprouts or turnips?

Unlike addictive smoking and abusive drinking,
sexual abuse of children does not involve a chemically addictive substance.
Like the compulsive behavior of overeating, sexual abuse of children *does*
include parts that are emotionally and physically rewarding and reinforce
the behavior. One of the strongest reinforcers of sexual behavior is *orgasm*, a
highly pleasurable physical sensation related to the release of sex tensions in
the body. Child sexual abusers get feelings of *power* through *control* of the
child (or children) and others and through achieving *sexual pleasure* in this
way.[2] The pleasurable feelings released during orgasm can reinforce sexually abusive behavior, but they do not cause sexual abuse of children. Those
same feelings can be released by healthy sexual activities. So again, child
sexual abusers *choose* to express their sexual feelings by using children
instead of by sharing relationships with people their own age or even by
pleasuring themselves (masturbating).

Sexual abuse of children *is* about power and control, but does it make any
sense to say that sexual abuse is *not* also about sex?

- Could we say that alcohol abuse is *not* about alcohol?
- Or drug abuse is *not* about drugs?
- Or smoking is *not* about cigarettes?
- Or overeating is *not* about food?

That would be like saying that eating chocolate cake is
not about eating chocolate.

49

Notes

1. Pithers, W. D., Kashima, K., Cumming, G., Beal, L., & Buell, M. (1988). Relapse prevention of sexual aggression. In R. A. Prentky & V. I. Quinsey (Eds.), *Human sexual aggression: Current perspectives*. New York: New York Academy of Sciences.
2. Hindman, J. (1989). *Just before dawn*. Ontario, Ore.: AlexAndria Associates.

section III: understanding the abused child in the family

6

Why Abusers Choose Particular Children

As we have discussed, many abusers use excuses for their behavior that include blaming the victim. They might say the child wanted the sexual touching and started it. Many people who sexually touch children try to convince themselves and everyone else that they abused only one child, that there was something special about that *particular* child, and that they could never do it to anyone else. If they abused a stepchild, they might say that they would never do it to their biological child. Or they might say that they did it to their stepchild only because he or she had always been sexual, even when young. They might say it happened because of the way the child dressed. If an adolescent abused a younger child while babysitting, the teenager might say that he or she would never sexually abuse his or her own sister or brother.

Most abusers want to believe that they are able to maintain control and act safely around children. More important, they want everyone else to think of them as safe around children. Also, to avoid taking full responsibility, some abusers want everyone to believe that the sexually abusive behavior was partly the child's fault because of some problem in the child's character or the child's personality or the way the child dressed or behaved.

Does that kind of thinking really make sense? To think like this, a person would have to believe that the child had special magnetic powers that pulled the abuser to him or her. Even if we could imagine a child having such magnetism, the child still could attract only someone who *already* had the ability to be sexually attracted to a child.

That's how magnets work. Think about it. When you put a magnet near metals that have iron in them, the magnet immediately attaches to the object. But when you put a magnet near other non-iron metals, like aluminum or copper, the magnet does not work. No matter how close you place them to each other, the magnet can't attract the non-iron metal.

It is the quality inside the metal that determines whether the magnet attracts the object. It is the same in situations of sexual abuse. It is the quality inside the abuser, not inside the child, that determines whether the child attracts the sexual desires of the abuser.

Think about the child who was abused in your family. *Many* people have been near this child, but only people with sexual touching problems actually abused this child. Think about yourself, if you are *not* the abuser: why didn't *you* sexually abuse this child, too?

Probably even as you are reading these words, you are reacting with anger or disgust. You know that you could never even think of sexually abusing a child. Clearly, sexual abuse does *not* occur because of particular qualities of the child who was abused. Sexual abuse occurs solely because of particular qualities of the *abuser*. Sexual abuse occurs because of the distorted way the *abuser* thinks.

It is true that, sometimes, victims of abuse might unthinkingly put themselves in situations where they are at high risk for sexual assault. Teenagers might walk down a deserted street alone at night, or vulnerable adults might go into a bar alone. They might go someplace with someone they do not know well. They might not choose relationships carefully and end up with someone who is more aggressive, possibly even violent, than they realized. These situations present risk of harm for *adults* and *some older adolescents*. It is important to remember, however, that even when people put themselves at high risk for abuse or assault, that does *not* mean that they wanted it to happen or that it is their fault. It *does* mean that they need to learn how to avoid high-risk situations. Adults need to be responsible for their own safety whenever possible.

Children also need to learn how to avoid high-risk situations if they can, such as staying away from a relative or friend who has a sexual touching problem, but *children* should never be held responsible for their own sexual abuse. Both inside and outside the family, it is always the *adult's* responsibility not to abuse a child, no matter how old the child is. Outside the family, children should not have to worry about whether their classroom at school or their scout troop or their camp is a *high-risk* situation. Inside the family, certainly no child should ever have to worry that his or her home is a *high-risk* situation for sexual abuse. Children do not choose where they live or where they go to school. Children often can't control who they are around, such as in family, camp, or babysitting situations. Adults in the family have created the environment in which the children find themselves. It is up to the adults at home to provide safety so that children can grow up learning to trust the people who care for them.

There are also *good qualities* about the child that abusers take advantage of in order to get what they want.[1] For example, if an abuser knows that the child is caring and loving, the abuser might say, "If you go along with this [sexual abuse], then I'll really know how much you love me." If an abuser knows that the child is worried about a depressed parent, such as the mother, the abuser might say, "We have to keep our secret. I know you wouldn't want to make Mom more unhappy." If an abuser knows that the child loves both parents and is afraid they won't stay together, the abuser might say, "You're special to me. This is our secret. Don't tell your dad, or he might get so upset that we'd get a divorce." If an abuser knows that the child loves to laugh and play, the abuser might make the sexual abuse appear like a game, such as wrestling or tickling or a "truth or dare" game.

Even though an abuser may have taken advantage of a child's good qualities, those good qualities are still valuable and important. To teach a child how to keep safe from abuse, it is helpful to understand how the abuser took advantage of and used those qualities to get the child involved in the sexual activity and the secret-keeping. Children should not carry shame or responsibility for their own abuse. To grow healthy and strong, children need and deserve adults who will help them find ways to feel proud of themselves, not ashamed.

Why Children Can't Just Say "No" and Tell Someone

Some children tell someone right away about secret sexual touching, and the person they tell gets the abuse to stop. Many children, however, are unable to tell for lots of different reasons. Children may be confused; they may enjoy feeling special and important to the abuser; they may think they are to blame; they may be afraid; they may be protecting another family member from harm. Children may be trapped in a situation where they feel they have no choice.

The abuser often uses a variety of methods to gain control of the relationship with the abused child: offers of a special relationship, bribes with special treats, or threats of extreme consequences. The abuser may make himself or herself even more important to the abused child by convincing the child that their relationship is special and full of extra love, while at the same time trying to turn that child away from other people in the family.

When offering a special relationship is the approach, the abusing person might say something like, "If your father loved you as much as I do, wouldn't he pay a little more attention to you?" Or, "Your brother is such an aggravating jerk, I don't know how you can stand to be around him." The adult abuser might even play on the child's sympathies with statements like, "I know this [the abusive sexual touching] is wrong and I know I have a problem, but your mother doesn't understand me or love me like you do. You're the only one I can count on to help me with my problem."

When bribery with special treats is the approach, an adolescent abuser might offer something like, "When you're brave enough to do this with me, then I'll know you've got the guts to join my club" or ". . . then I'll be able to let you use my new computer game." When threats of the family falling apart is the approach, the abuser might say something like, "If your mother found out about us, it would kill her" or ". . . she'd just leave the family."

The abuser uses these approaches to build up the wall of secrecy around the sexual activity and to draw the child away from close relationships with others in the family. Children usually become confused about what to do with the mixed messages inside their minds. They may believe that the abuser is right and that their relationship is special. They may also know that the secret sexual activity is wrong and do not want to participate. But they may fear that if they fight back against the abuser, they will lose everything.

All these conflicting messages can cause a great deal of confusion and turmoil inside the child's mind. This is especially so when the older person giving the controlling messages is someone the child admires or loves. When children are convinced that they can't escape ongoing sexual abuse, they often *adjust* to the situation *in order to survive*. This process of eventually adjusting to the demands of the abuser is often referred to as the *accommodation syndrome*.[2] The child temporarily puts aside his or her own needs and conflicting feelings in order to go along with the requests of the abuser. This *accommodation* process is very similar to what adults go through when they've been captured and held for a long time, such as in concentration camps or during kidnappings, or even in some cult groups that draw people away from their families.[3] The captured person becomes emotionally attached to and dependent on the person who controls whether and when he or she eats, sleeps, exercises, uses a bathroom, and receives mail, or is isolated, beaten, or emotionally abused.

In a similar way, the "captured" person in a family — the abused child — can become emotionally attached to and dependent on the abusing person, who often controls whether and when the child has friends, participates in school activities, gets to use the computer or pick television shows or receive phone calls, sleeps through the night, or is isolated, beaten, or emotionally abused.

This process of finding a way to live in and accept an *unacceptable* situation often keeps children from telling, as they are caught in a whirlpool of confusing feelings about their abuser. They can fear and love the abuser at the same time. Children can be hurt, abused, and traumatized while in these strong, confusing relationships controlled by the abuser. This emotional and psychological connection to the abuser and the abuse is referred to as a *trauma bond*, which can continue long after the abuse has stopped.[4] Sometimes memories of the abuse, with their mixture of emotional, mental, and physical feelings, seem to stick with abused children, no matter how hard they want to get rid of the thoughts and feelings.

Let's look even closer into how this powerful yet confusing relationship develops between abuser and child. Even if the child cannot understand what happened or why the abuser gained control, it's important for the protecting adults to understand the many ways children become powerless. If protecting adults can help a child understand the child's powerlessness in the relationship with the abuser, they can help the child feel less shamed by his or her involvement in past abuse and more able to protect himself or herself from abusive relationships in the future.

There are *natural qualities* about children that make it easy for abusers to sexually abuse them. The child is smaller, younger, or in other respects less powerful than the abuser. There are also *natural qualities* about the abuser that make abuse possible. Adults and older adolescents are physically bigger. Adults also are in positions of power, as they should be, to guide, to nurture, to protect, and to teach children to obey and respect rules of authority.

Parents do not tell their children, "Obey me sometimes, but not all the time." When parents put an older child in charge as a babysitter, they do not tell their younger children, "It is okay for you to decide when to obey the babysitter." Parents teach their young children to obey *all* the time. Given all this, how are young children supposed to know that they should *disobey* an older person who tricks them into participating in sexual abuse?

The abuser takes advantage of these natural conditions and natural qualities to control the child. *This is not the fault of the child.* It is helpful to look at photographs or just think of the abused child standing next to the person who committed the abuse. Which one do you think is stronger? Who is more able to control the other?

Children are often *confused* about what happened, because abusers sometimes touch them in such a way that the children do not know for sure how it happened. They may not be sure if someone abused them or if it was all just an accident or part of a game. The child *may* feel right away that this kind of sexual touching by the abuser is wrong. Yet the child may become confused because someone he or she loves or trusts or has been told to obey is the one performing the sexual behavior.

The child is also confused by the way the abuser gains control through a process called *grooming*.[5] The abuser gradually gains the child's trust or love, while at the same time increasingly exposing the child to sexual ideas, images, or touch. It is done in such a confusing, secret way that the child is not quite aware of what is happening but knows it is secret.

Another part of the grooming pattern includes the abuser's use of *thinking errors* to trick the child and to change the child's way of thinking. In this way the abuser teaches the child to use *thinking errors* in order to handle staying in the relationship with the abuser. For example, a child might think, "It must really be okay, because he would never do anything to hurt me." Or, "I'm special, she said so. I'm the man of the family now." Or, "It's not really bad. He's not forcing me to do it."

Most children cannot bear to even think of the word *abuse* (even when they've learned it in school) in connection with the parent or friend or other favorite relative who is such fun a lot of the time and does those "weird things" only some of the time. The abuser might give the child such special feelings, both emotional and physical, that the child does not want to stop. Remember that the abuser may have tricked the child into believing that this is a special way to love him or her.

Often children are tricked into believing that the abuse is *their* fault because they are cooperating with the abuser. Abusers are likely to use words that trick the child into thinking that it is a shared activity and a shared responsibility. Instead of saying "I *forced* sex onto the child," for example, abusers might say, "*Let's* do it!" or "*We* had sex *together*" or "I had sex *with* the child." Abusers use these trick words to try to avoid taking total responsibility for their own behavior. Sometimes when the child accepts gifts or money before or after the touching, the child might think, "Well, I wanted that remote control car . . ." or "I let him take me out for pizza . . . so I must have wanted the touching." Abusers want to trick the child and everyone around them into forgetting that a child is too young to make decisions about sex. *It is always the adult's or older person's responsibility to NOT sexually touch a child.*

It is no wonder children get confused about whether they are responsible for their own abuse. Without meaning to, even well-intentioned adults sometimes send that message to children. Most sexual abuse prevention programs in schools or on TV, for example, emphasize the importance of the child saying no to any sexual advances and of telling a safe adult. This sends the message that somehow the child might be able to control the situation if he or she could only speak up. While it is wise and appropriate to encourage the child not to keep any secrets about abuse, it just doesn't make sense to put pressure on a child when it is the adult who has the problem. In other situations when the adults clearly have the problem, such as drinking and driving, the media pressure is clearly on the adult not to drink and drive. There are no TV commercials suggesting that it is the child's responsibility to refuse to get into his or her drunk parent's car. What is missing in the media and in sexual abuse prevention programs is a commercial that sends a message to abusers not to sexually abuse children.

Although people can usually understand how qualities of size and power give abusers an advantage over young children, they often have a hard time recognizing those same qualities when the victim is an older child or teenager. Sometimes a teenage child looks like an adult or acts more sexually sophisticated than other kids that age. Even in these situations, it is always important to ask the same question about the abuser-victim relationship as we would when the power difference is more obvious: is this an equal relationship, or one in which one person is stronger and more able to control the other? It is also important to learn how long the abuser has controlled the relationship. Often the teenager has been a victim for years and learned at an early age that his or her strongest value to others was being sexual.

Many teenagers who disclose their victimization have experienced the powerlessness and confusion of sexual abuse, by one or by many abusers, since they were small children. In fact, sometimes it is only as the children grow older that they understand more clearly the abusive quality of the relationship, and they become more determined to find a way out by telling someone. This is, however, an extremely difficult thing to do.

Unfortunately, older children often mistakenly believe that both the abuse and keeping it secret for a long time are partly their fault. They do not recognize how the abuser *groomed* them or forced them to *accommodate* to the abuser's demands. Rather than finding it easier to tell as they get older, some children grow more afraid that terrible things will happen if everyone learns their shameful secret. They may fear that everyone will judge them and consider them bad and that no one will love them. This is especially true in situations in which the abuser has controlled the abused child and the situation for so long that the child has lost emotional closeness to other siblings or to the nonabusing parent or parents.

Summing It Up

Because it is so important to be absolutely clear about who is responsible for sexual behavior between adults and children, here's a review of some of the material from the preceding section.

Remember that when children disclose information about their abuse, they want to stop the sexual touching, the confusion, the discomfort, and the secrecy around the abuse, but they do not want to make people they love sad or angry. Children often keep quiet because they are confused and unsure, because they are afraid they will get into trouble, or because they are afraid they might lose someone's love.

Sometimes when they first learn of the sexual abuse, family members *do* get angrier at the victim than at the abuser. This is exactly what the abuser said would happen, so it is no wonder children blame themselves.

Remember the strongest fear that often keeps children quiet: if they tell, it would be their fault if the abuser had to move out of the home or even went to jail, or if their parents got divorced, or if their family broke up, or if the abused child was placed in foster care.

So does it make sense that children would lie when they tell about being sexually abused? Does it make sense that children would make up something to bring so much trouble on themselves? If the child loves the abuser, does it make sense that the child would make up something that would cause the abuser to be taken away? If the child is scared or uneasy around the abuser, does it make sense that the child would lie in such a way as to make that person angry?

If children are angry at or don't like someone, it *is* possible that they *might* make up a story about sexual activity with that person. But in these situations, it is less likely that children would tell a lie that would embarrass or shame them and that might cause others to blame them for participating. It is less likely that children would make up details about embarrassing behavior that they would have to repeat over and over to authorities.

Why Children Often Tell Someone Outside the Family

Sometimes children tell someone in their own families about the sexual abuse, but often they tell someone outside the family. Parents may feel hurt or angry that their child did not tell them first. There are many reasons children do not feel able to tell even the best parents about the abuse.

Remember that the abuser may have tricked the child into believing that he or she would lose the family's love. Parents teach their children to both give and receive love. Children grow up needing this love and care in their homes. Children, therefore, may be afraid to do something that might cause them to lose the love of people who are important to them.

An even stronger force keeping the child from telling the nonabusing parents may be the child's fear that the information will cause too much emotional pain for the parents to bear. Some children say that they did not want to see their mothers cry, or their fathers be sad. So they do not tell in order to protect their parents from feeling sadness or pain.

Still, confusing thoughts and feelings usually grow inside these children, often getting so strong that they can't focus on other parts of their lives. A deep sadness, anger, or fear may keep them from concentrating on their schoolwork or from performing well in other activities. When the feelings get too strong, children may not be able to keep them inside. The feelings may come out in many ways, sometimes through aggressive behavior or depression.

As the children start *acting out* their feelings, they may behave in ways that make it hard for other kids or adults to be with them. Sometimes the feelings of confusion, anger, fear, or sadness grow so strong that children look for someone to talk to, someone that they can tell without worrying about hurting them or losing their love. Children often tell their secret to someone outside their family, such as a friend, teacher, or guidance counselor.

Notes

1. Hindman, J. (1989). *Just before dawn.* Ontario, Ore.: AlexAndria Associates.

2. Summit, R.C. (1983). The child abuse accommodation syndrome. *Child Abuse and Neglect, 7,* 177–193.

3. Herman, J. (1992). *Trauma and recovery.* New York: Basic Books.

4. Herman, J. (1992). *Trauma and recovery.* New York: Basic Books.

   Hindman, J. (1991). *The mourning breaks: 101 "proactive" treatment strategies for breaking the trauma bonds of sexual abuse.* Ontario, Ore.: AlexAndria Associates.

5. Berliner, L., & Conte, J. R. (1990). The process of victimization: The victim's perspective. *Child Abuse and Neglect, 14*(1), 29–40.

   Conte, J. R., Wolf, S., & Smith, T. (1989). What sexual offenders tell us about prevention strategies. *Child Abuse and Neglect, 13*(2), 293–301.

7

Who's to Blame?

Is anyone *other* than the abuser to blame? No. Abusers are responsible for the sexual abuse. They set up the whole situation in order to control people in their families. They *weave a web of secrecy and control* and make the consequences for telling so serious that it is hard for anyone to stop them. It takes a great deal of courage for someone to tell about the abuse. Since abusers rarely stop their hurtful, controlling behavior by themselves, someone has to do something to make the abuse stop.

Invisible, Secret Webs

Even though the abuser is responsible for the sexual abuse, it is important to question what made the abuser's manipulations work. What was going on inside each person and inside your family as a whole? Why weren't adult family members able to protect the child? To understand how an abuser uses

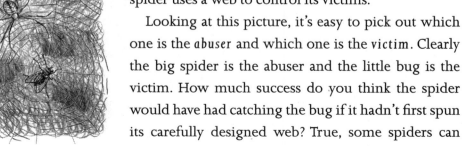

a web of secrecy to control others, let's look at how a spider uses a web to control its victims.

Looking at this picture, it's easy to pick out which one is the *abuser* and which one is the *victim*. Clearly the big spider is the abuser and the little bug is the victim. How much success do you think the spider would have had catching the bug if it hadn't first spun its carefully designed web? True, some spiders can catch bugs without webs, but most spiders use webs to catch their prey. Why do they use webs? Spider webs are finely woven and barely visible, yet they are quite strong. They can withstand rain and wind. They can just stay there waiting for bugs to come along. The web would be useless, however, if it were lying loosely on the ground. If you look closely, you'll notice that each point of the web is attached someplace with strong stuff like glue—the same stuff that makes the web stay together—the same sticky stuff that the spider uses to spin around its victim. Spiders can build webs only in places where there are just the right conditions for attaching a web. They might build a web on the corner of a porch post, for example, because they know the web will stick there. It's not the fault of the post that the web is there. The spider just took advantage of the post's natural qualities that make it good for sticking.

Sexual abusers often work like spiders, except the webs they spin are *invisible webs* made up of secrets and tricks that control and bind family members together. A few abusers sexually use children without a secret web, but most abusers in families need this kind of web in order to get away with their sexual abusing. Because the abuser's web is invisible, family members don't always know that it is there. Like the spider, however, the abuser can spin the web of secrecy only where the conditions are just right for attaching this kind of web. If the conditions are not right, the abuser will work to change things. When conditions are just right, the abuser can attach a corner of the secret web onto each person.

Let's look at some examples of how this invisible, secret web might work. An abuser might be able to spin an invisible web of manipulation around a nonabusing parent, perhaps one who already has a feeling of "low self-confidence" or "fear of being unable to make it without the abuser." If the parent becomes suspicious and asks questions, the abuser might be able to get that parent to back off by saying something (spinning the invisible web) that would attach to those exact feelings (low self-confidence and fear). For example, the abuser could say (spinning the web), "Who are *you* to question *me*? You have such a sick mind! I am tired of all your nagging. Get off my back!"

Let's think about situations in which a brother or sister (also called a *sibling*) might be suspicious that sexual abuse is going on but does not say anything. Abusers usually have worked to create a certain feeling inside the siblings so that they are afraid to tell. Abusers might say or do something (spinning the invisible web) that attaches to the sibling's feelings. For example, in everyday situations of control, abusers might use a high level of anger, maybe even violence such as punching a hole in the wall or hitting someone, to get people to obey. Or abusers might tell a child that the family will fall apart if anyone tells. Thus the sibling, as well as the abused child, has the right condition (fear of being hurt or of the parents divorcing) for the abuser to keep control and spin the secret web.

So you can see how the abuser's manipulations work like an invisible web, controlling not only the abused child, but also the other members of the family. This does *not* mean that anyone else *causes* the abuse by having a corner of the invisible control web attached to them. This is an important point: it is the abuser who creates or takes advantage of each person's "condition" in order to fasten the invisible web of secrets and manipulations. Before the abuse can stop and stay stopped, the abuser has to figure out and explain to the rest of the family just what kinds of tricks and manipulations he or she used to make sure that the invisible, secret web stayed strong.

The nonabusing parents or caretakers also have an important task in treatment: to figure out their own emotional and mental conditions that might have allowed the abuser to more easily attach a secret, invisible web. If they can know this about themselves, the nonabusing parents or caretakers can figure out what things they can change and new ways to protect themselves and their children in the future. Spouses or parents of the abuser, for example, might learn how to have more confidence in themselves so that they do not back away from their suspicions when they *know* something is wrong.

The family has an important task: to locate all the people who might have been tricked into letting the abuser attach a corner of the secret web — spouses, partners, children, grandparents, friends — and explain how it happened. Once everyone knows the abuser's tricks as well as their own personal "conditions," the abuser will have a hard time fooling anyone in the family the same way again.

Not All Webs Are Dangerous

An important thing to remember is that it's natural for webs to develop in families and in our lives in general. Webs of emotions and beliefs and thoughts connect us to one another and to other important events and resources and goals. The World Wide Web connects people all over the world who are interested in books or antiques or astronomy or who want support in dealing with a problem or a disease.

But for webs to be a positive way of connecting, they cannot be secret and invisible and controlling. Let's think about how *visible, open, connecting webs* can be spun in families to support the emotional, psychological, and physical needs of individuals and of the family as a whole.

One of the most positive ways that a web is spun in a family is by parents caring for their children, not just physically but by teaching them their values and beliefs. Families develop certain codes that become part of the visible web that binds them together. Some examples of positive codes are a "code of honesty," a "code of caring," and a "code of togetherness."

Parents support these codes by insisting that their children always tell the truth, by providing appropriate discipline, by teaching their children to do kind things for others, and by making an effort to spend time together having fun, working on projects, or solving problems. Holiday traditions are an obvious example of the positive visible web being spun among all members of the family, even those who live outside the home: cards are sent, gifts are given, meals are shared, and time is spent together.

Hard times, such as family illness or death, also highlight the positive visible web. Family members can help one another get through the emotional and physical demands of coping with the situation.

Without some sort of weaving together of lives, like in a web, people would have a hard time being connected to one another and feeling supported in their lives. Family stories are a popular web-spinning way to share what happens to each member, to bring events from the past into the present, and to develop a sense of family history. For example, children often hear stories about their parents and grandparents that happened long before they were born. And grandparents who live far away might hear stories about events in their grandchildren's lives.

For children and families to grow healthy and strong, they need visible, open webs connecting members to one another. When sexual abuse occurs in a family, the abuser takes advantage of the natural need for families to develop webs. But there is a big difference between the *abuser's invisible, secret, control web* and the *family's visible, open, connecting web.*

8

Why the Whole Family Comes for Treatment: Abuse Is Everybody's Problem

We have looked at how a spider's web is attached at many different points, just as an abuser's invisible, secret, control web may be attached to many different people. Let's look again at the spider web to help us understand why it makes sense for the whole family to be involved in treatment.

We could catch the spider and make it take classes to learn not to pick on little bugs. We could rescue the little bug and bring it in for treatment, where it could talk about its feelings and learn to protect itself. But what would happen to each of them when they went back home? The invisible, secret, control web would still be there. If no one else in the bug's family came in for treatment, none of the other bugs in the family would learn about spider webs and how dangerous they can be.

And you know how bugs are — mother bugs and baby bugs — they like to climb around things all day long, looking for food. That's natural for bugs to do. Chances are good that those bugs would climb right into that web and get stuck there.

Imagine the spider coming back home and seeing its web still in place. Do you think the spider could resist catching another bug? The web is still all set up for the spider to go back into the bug-catching business. That is natural for spiders to do. Maybe the little bug will know *how* to stay away from the spider, but what is a little bug to do if the rest of its bug family is still crawling near that web?

Perhaps this particular spider is no longer around. Maybe it went to another part of the woods to live forever. What do you suppose another spider coming along might do if it found this beautifully woven web, all ready to move into?

It would be quite easy for this new spider to start catching all the bugs around — even the little bug who was in treatment. Why? Well, the little bug's family thought that the problem was just between that little bug and one particular spider. None of the other little bugs in the family went for treatment, so they never learned about the secret control web or about other spiders. They keep on playing near the invisible web. In fact, they are so busy just being bugs that they don't notice the web at all. After a while, even the little bug is tired of being left out and wants to join its family.

Of course, there is a difference between spiders and human sexual abusers. Spiders can't change — they have to make webs to catch and eat bugs in order to survive. Many sexual abusers, in contrast, *can* choose to change; they do not *need* sex with children to survive. And your family definitely does not live in a spider web. But it does live within another kind of web that the abuser in your family has been weaving — that invisible, secret, web of manipulation, control, and misuse of power.

Sometimes it's hard to get everyone in a family to come in for treatment. That's understandable, considering how hard it is to think about sexual abuse. Some family members want to avoid the problem, some are confused or frightened, some are too angry or hurt, and some may think the abuse has nothing to do with them. Sometimes families can still learn about secret, abuse-producing webs as long as the nonabusing adults in each family come to treatment to learn as much as they can about how to prevent abuse. Then these nonabusing adults can change the way things are at home — by being aware of any signs of abuse, opening up communication in the family, believing and supporting the child who was abused, holding the abusing person responsible for the abuse, and learning to confront distorted thinking and manipulative behavior.

It is easier, though, when the whole family comes in for treatment. Then everyone can learn together how to avoid being part of *any* abuser's secret, control web. And when a family learns together, each member can help watch out for the others.

It's Hard for Others to See What's Happening

It can hurt when you hear others say, "She must have known what was going on in her own home," or "It's hard to believe the other children didn't notice something." Some people do have the ability to figure out what's going on behind the scenes in lots of situations. They learn to read people's faces for reactions, are aware of body language, and notice lots of clues about what's going on. Yet family members often are not aware that sexual abuse is occurring in their own family. Sometimes they seem to notice that *something* is going on, but they act as if they didn't see a thing.

This reaction can be very confusing for children who believe, or have been told, that parents know *everything*. When the child didn't feel well or was sad or troubled about something at school or with friends, the parent took one look at the child and asked, "What's wrong?" That child probably didn't have to say anything — the parent just knew there was a problem. So when the nonabusing parent does not seem to react to the abuse situation, the child may think either that the nonabusing parent doesn't have any idea what's going on or that the nonabusing parent *can* see what's going on and that it's okay.

People often have a hard time facing difficult situations and dealing with painful emotions such as fear, anxiety, and anger. When families have to struggle to face the reality that sexual abuse is occurring, they might fight against believing it. They want the family to survive. They might be afraid that if they face the truth, the consequences will be too hard to bear. There is a strong *code of loyalty* in most families. Sometimes the code sounds like "Family comes first" or "Don't talk about family matters outside the family." "Don't air dirty linen" is another family saying. Loyalty is important for keeping families together, because members support, protect, and take care of one another. In families where sexual abuse occurs, however, the abusers manipulate and take advantage of family loyalty: not talking about family matters is exactly what sexual abusers want, so they can continue their behavior.

Breaking the *code of silence* is difficult for both children and adults. They usually fear that there will be a big price to pay. They may fear getting in trouble for talking, for being part of the abuse, or for not stopping the abuse. They may fear that the whole family will fall apart, either through divorce or by someone having to move out of the home. These fears are particularly strong if the abuser has made threats about punishment or divorce. Everyone in the family is caught in a trap: if they have to face the truth about what is happening, they have to deal with some tough feelings and decisions.

Remember that some members of a family might not be aware of the sexual abuse at all, because the abuser has been clever at hiding his or her abusive behavior. Others in the family may pick up on "signals" inside themselves that something is wrong. However, there seems to be no way to survive and keep the family together if they tell, so they learn to block out the information about sexual abuse and ignore any signals that danger exists.

Another way to think of it is that because child sexual abuse usually occurs within a relationship, the child's normal learning about trusting, secure, stable relationships may be disrupted.[1] We might think of this natural ability to distinguish between safe and dangerous relationships as a person's radar. We all are born with this radar. In families where sexual abuse occurs, however, the radar is jammed and the signals are scrambled. Something wrong is happening, but when adults don't respond, children in the family learn to ignore their own radar.

Perhaps the story in the following metaphor will illustrate how radar stops being effective.

Unreliable Radar

Think of a large ship that relies on its radar to travel safely through the ocean. Imagine that the radar has picked up the signal of a small boat directly in front of the large ship. The crew members are below deck under the watchful supervision of the Second in Command. They all think they hear a "ping" noise from the radar screen, but then they hear the Captain order, "Full speed ahead!" They're confused

for a minute, but they've always trusted the Captain, so they return to their work. The large ship plows right through the small boat, breaking it into many pieces and hurting the people in the boat. The ship jolts ever so slightly. But it's a huge ship and a very little boat, so the big ship just continues steadily on its way.

The crew members feel vibrations and hear something like the muffled voices of people screaming. They run to the top deck, but the Captain angrily orders them back to their jobs, saying that everything is "just fine." The crew turns to see the nervous Second in Command pausing at the entrance to the deck and starting to speak: "Captain, I . . ."

Staring straight ahead, the Captain angrily repeats his words, "I said, everything is just fine." The Second in Command returns below deck, but somehow he can't meet the eyes of the crew. "Okay, now, back to business. You heard the Captain." The crew is confused and upset: they're almost sure they felt something. But the Second in Command doesn't seem **that** concerned, and after all, the Captain is the only one who can actually see what's going on. Gradually, they return to work.

Before long, the crew members are sure they hear another "ping" from the radar screen. Surely, they think, this time the Captain will pay attention to the radar and stop the ship. Instead, the crew again hears the Captain shout, "Full speed ahead!"

The crew looks to the Second in Command, who takes a deep breath, summons up his courage, and goes up on the top deck. "Captain, have you heard the radar warning for the small boat?"

The Captain turns and furrows his brow deeply, his eyes blazing with anger. "Are you questioning my authority?"

he bellows. "If you ever do that again, you will be fired from your command." The Captain darts over to the radar machine and turns down the volume of the warning signals.

Feeling powerless to argue with the Captain, the Second in Command retreats and quickly goes below deck. He again avoids eye contact with the anxious crew members while he barks out orders, "All right, now. Stop slacking off and get back to work. You heard the Captain." The crew members draw back, away from their Second in Command. They return to washing the floors and polishing the brass rails, even as they feel a sudden jolt followed by vibrations. They hear muffled sounds in the distance but are not quite sure what's happening.

Hours later, the Captain summons the Second in Command and the crew to the top deck for a drill. By this time, there are no signs of any crash. There are a few little boats in the area, but they all look fine. The Captain compliments them all on the fine job they did below deck. He tells them that he may give them extra time off on shore and a bonus when they pull into the next port.

The next day another small boat is crossing the path of the great ship. The sound of the radar "pings" are only faintly heard by the crew members, who are again below deck. They look at one another, but then gradually go back to work. No one says anything. The Second in Command just stares down at the deck. They hear the Captain's loud footsteps as he crosses the deck to turn the sound of the radar machine completely off. "Full speed ahead!" they all hear. Then they feel a slight jolt, followed by vibrations, and barely hear the sounds of muffled voices. They look anxiously at each other and at the Second in Command, who starts for the stairs, pauses, and then returns to his own command post.

Later that day when the radar "pings" noiselessly, the crew members hear nothing. They have been anxious and irritable all day and are slow to respond to orders from their Second in Command. A fight breaks out, and the crew doesn't feel the jolt or the vibrations or hear the sounds as the big ship crashes through yet another small boat.

The sexual abuser in a family works much like this bullying Captain. The abuser takes advantage of his or her position of authority and uses certain techniques to keep control. Most members of abusive families don't just stand by and watch the abuse happen. Like the Second in Command and crew on the ship, however, they are in an unequal relationship with the person who has the power. They may depend on the financial support provided by the abuser. They may feel threatened or powerless to argue with the abuser. They may be rewarded (or bribed) with special treatment for keeping quiet. When they no longer feel that they can count on the nonabusing adults to control the situation, family members often become irritable with one another and disrespectful of the nonabusing adults.

Over time, the abuser becomes clever at manipulating others and hiding the secret behavior. The abuser is able to reduce the alarm signals from the child who is being abused, as well as those from the family's radar that something is wrong. Family members' trust in their own instincts and in their ability to speak up grows weaker each time there is no response that tells them that their radar is working well and that the signals are important. They do not hear, "Yes, something is wrong and the adults will fix the problem." Family members may learn to ignore any signals their radar puts out. Over time, their radar may not pick up any signals, either inside the family or outside in the larger social world.

Dissociation: Like a Horse Wearing Blinders

It's hard to understand how anyone could miss something that is happening right in front of him or her, but sexual abuse does not usually happen that way. It happens out of direct sight. Let's think about another situation where it's not possible to see what's going on.

Have you ever seen a horse being led down a busy street, maybe in a parade? The owner knows that horses, with their eyes designed to take it all in, are naturally curious about and interested in what goes on around them. So the horse won't be distracted by all the sights and sounds of the street, the owner puts blinders on the horse.

Although the horse is able to hear sounds, it can't quite figure out where they're coming from, so it ignores everything and just walks on.

These blinders allow the owner to control what the horse sees and how it responds to what it hears. The blinders keep the horse from seeing things that might cause it to run wild. They allow the owner to keep control over the horse.

Remember, the horse did not ask for blinders. In fact, it may not even know it's wearing blinders. Thus the owner tricks the horse into acting as if nothing is going on around it.

In families where sexual abuse occurs, the abuser tricks the family members into wearing their own invisible "blinders." The family members do not even realize that they are wearing blinders. Their blinders have developed over time as they have been taught by experience to ignore the warnings when their own internal radar senses danger. Since their warning systems are not working well, the nonabused children and the nonabusing parents or caretakers are not aware of or do not know how to respond to the abuse. So sometimes they do not react at all. They have been tricked into acting like nothing is going on around them. Remember, the abuser does not want the other family members to run wild and get angry or tell the authorities. In this way, the blinders in the family serve the abuser, but they do not protect the children.

Sometimes wearing blinders seems like the only way to get through the day, to survive an abusive situation. A child may develop his or her own blinders in order to have a life outside the abuse. When the abused child goes to school, for example, the last thing the child wants to remember or think about is the sexual abuse that is going on at home. Children want to be able to be with friends, to do schoolwork, or to participate in music or sports. Children can't do a good job at any of those tasks if they are worried or saddened or scared by sexual abuse. The child protects himself or herself from those feelings by blocking out all thoughts about the abuse. It is as if the child were wearing blinders through life.

Sometimes parents of abused children grew up in their own abusive environments. This may mean that since they were young, they learned to put on blinders and not see things that made them unhappy or afraid. They learned to look straight ahead and to ignore all the upsetting thoughts that came into their minds.

During ongoing sexual abuse, radar may break down, blinders may get bigger, and feelings of powerlessness may take over and drain the energy out of life. Children may find themselves in situations that seem to have no solution. When children are living under these conditions for too long, they may learn to survive the awful situation through a process called *dissociation*.[2] Their bodies are there, but their minds are somewhere else. For a short while, it is almost as if they are not aware that someone is abusing them.

Most of us dissociate a little bit in everyday life in boring situations or during circumstances that have become routine. Have you ever been in a situation where you couldn't escape having to listen to someone talk, such as sitting in a classroom or attending a lecture? Perhaps you *daydreamed* about doing something fun later in the day. Your mind went somewhere else, and you missed everything the person was saying.

Have you ever been so busy thinking about other things while driving that you were not aware of where you were and missed your turn? You might have said, "My mind was somewhere else."

These are the kinds of everyday *dissociation* that we all experience once in a while. Abused children who feel unable to change their situation may learn to use dissociation over and over just to get through the sexual abuse experience. The more children use dissociation, the more powerful it can become as a method for coping with painful or unhappy situations.

A child who learns to manage life by dissociating (putting on emotional or mental blinders) can grow up to become a parent who manages life by dissociating. Because these adults have been wearing blinders for so long, they do not even realize they are wearing them. Parents with blinders either are unable to pick up clear signals that sexual abuse is going on or feel powerless to do anything about it. Parents with these ways of coping are usually not able to protect children from abuse.

Fortunately, wearing blinders or having unreliable radar does not have to be a lifelong problem. With help in treatment, family members can learn how to deal with the sad and angry and hurt feelings that come up when they think about sexual abuse happening in their family. They can take off their blinders and get their radar working again. They can learn new ways to see things clearly and new ways to make sure that all children are safe in their own homes.

The Abuse Has Stopped: "Why Can't We Just Go Back to Normal?"

You may wish that all the protective authorities and treatment providers would just let your family go back to normal, to the way it was before the disclosure of abuse. If you think hard about it, however, you will realize that "back to normal" was how things were *while* the abuse was occurring. "Normal" in your family meant that someone was abusing a child and that the child may not have dared to tell anyone about it. "Normal" in your family meant that some of you knew about it, and some of you did not, but none of you found a way to stop it before it happened. "Normal" in your family meant that the abuser had the ability to gain control over one or all of you. That person used many thinking errors or tricks to get what he or she wanted. It is important to talk about the tricks so that everyone will know them and no one can trick you that way again. If abusers learn to care more about their victims and their families than about protecting themselves, they can become honest in sharing information about the tricks they used to control you.

Let's compare the abuser's tricks to a magician's trick of separating three brass rings. At first, you can't see how he gets them apart. If the magician shows *one person* in the audience how he does the trick, that person won't be tricked again, but anyone else in the audience

74

can still be fooled. If he shows *everyone* how he does the trick, he won't be able to fool anyone the next time. If the magician shows all his tricks, he won't be able to have a show at all because he won't be able to trick anyone.

If abusers can show all their "tricks" of manipulation, they will have a much harder time tricking or abusing anyone again. This family awareness will both help keep children safe and help abusers keep their problem behaviors under control. Remember, the abuser's web is a lot like the spider's web: conditions have to be just right for the abuser (or the spider) to attach the web. Family awareness changes the conditions so that it becomes harder for the web to stick.

Anyone who has sexually abused a child has a lot of work to do in treatment in order to understand his or her own behaviors and thinking patterns. Before being allowed around children, abusers must figure out *why* they sexually abused a child — that is, what underlying emotional and psychological needs they were trying to meet. Then they must figure out *how* they set up the situation at home to control everyone. Then, if they work hard to learn new ways to control *themselves* instead of others — if they work hard to learn how to think more honestly and not use thinking errors — maybe they will be able to stop sexually abusing children. It is not easy to change behavior patterns that have been around for a long time.

Notes

1. Elliott, D. M. (1994). Impaired object relations in professional women molested as children. *Psychotherapy*, 31, 79–86.

2. Briere, J., & Conte, J. R. (1993). Self-reported amnesia for abuse in adults molested as children. *Journal of Traumatic Stress*, 6, 21–32.

   Williams, L. (1994). Recall of childhood trauma: A prospective study of women's memories of child sexual abuse. *Journal of Consulting and Clinical Psychology*, 62, 1167–1176.

part two

How Much Harm?

9

Recognizing the Hidden Injury

The disclosure or discovery of sexual abuse has torn like a storm through your heart and through the heart of your family. As after any storm, it is necessary to assess the damage and determine what is needed to set things right. We have already looked at some of the hows and whys underlying the behavior of the sexual abuser. We have looked at some of the ways sexually abused children might react and feel. We have explored some of the responses nonabusing parents and nonabused siblings might have to ongoing sexual abuse within the family. We have been looking at these hard-to-see, "hidden" workings of family members: thoughts, feelings, motivations, and responses. Abusers manipulate and take advantage of these hidden workings and cause harm beneath the surface of each person and of the family as a whole.

Not every child or every family reacts to or is harmed by the sexual abuse and its disclosure in the same way. There are many factors within the people involved and within the abuser-victim relationship that determine why some children and some families suffer a great deal while others seem to bounce back and become stronger than before the disclosure. An important part of helping the abused child recover from the effects of the abuse depends on understanding all the different factors through a careful *trauma assessment*.

Trauma Assessment: What Hurts?

An *assessment* means looking at how a person is doing, at the person's strengths and challenges. A *trauma assessment* looks at how a person or family is affected by some terrible experience (a trauma) and what those individuals might need to help them cope.

79

A trauma assessment (which is usually done by a clinical social worker or other therapist) is different from a *legal* assessment. Because many child sexual abuse cases do end up in the courts, it is important to understand this difference between the world of therapy and the world of the criminal justice system. Both worlds can feel extremely confusing and overwhelming in the beginning. Looking at the differences between these systems can be helpful in understanding their distinct but often connected approaches.

When assessing the seriousness of a child sexual abuse *crime* in cases that go to court, the law (the police, prosecutors, and judges) looks at several factors: the *age* of the child and of the perpetrator at the time of the abuse, how often the abuse was done (the *frequency*), over how long a period of time (the *duration*), whether the abuser used *force* or *terror* (the amount of *violence*), and how much the *abuse intruded into* the child's body (the *type of sexual activity*).[1]

In a therapeutic trauma assessment, the goal is to discover the amount of *psychological* and *emotional trauma* a sexually abused child has experienced. Therapists look at other factors in addition to the ones lawyers examine: the abuser's *standing* and *reputation* in the community; the *quality of the relationship* among the victim, the abuser, and the other family members; the *lack of predictability* about when and where the abuse occurred (that is, was it a set routine every Tuesday night, or could the child be abused almost anywhere almost anytime?); the overall *lack of a sense of safety* in the home; and the family's and the community's *initial response* to the disclosure.[2]

The *community standing* part has to do with whether the abuser is able to hide his or her manipulations and abusive ways well enough so that he or she looks good to others in the family and in the larger community. This false appearance, which might be called the "hypocrisy factor," helps the abuser look more believable than the victim: the better the abuser looks, the less the victim feels that he or she will be believed, and the more hopeless and isolated the victim feels.

The *initial response* factor has to do with whether the abused child gets the support of family and friends right away. For all children who experience a traumatic reaction to the abuse, a common part of the trauma is the feeling of *total powerlessness.*

Abusers Hurt Everyone, Including Themselves

Abusers not only hurt others; they also hurt themselves. Abusers hurt themselves and others at the core of their being, at the core of their *spirit*.[3] When we talk about a person's spirit, we are talking about the part of a person that holds feelings of joy as well as pain. Our spiritual part connects with others and determines the way we feel about ourselves, about our lives. When people give up caring about themselves or others, when they are depressed and have no energy to enjoy or cope with life, they seem to have lost their spirit: it's as if they have given up.

Whenever people behave in ways that fill them with shame, they rob themselves of pride, dignity, and self-respect, and they cause injury to their own and to others' spirits. When others discover their behavior, abusers' self-esteem often falls even lower than it was while they were abusing. Their lives feel out of control. For abusers to break their cycle of abuse, they have to change their overall feelings of shame about having out-of-control behavior to overall feelings of pride about learning to control their behavior. No one can give these feelings to abusers. They have to work hard to gain their own self-respect, as well as the respect and trust of others, if they truly want to live open, honest lives. They have to work hard to repair their own spirits and the spirits of their victims and the families.

This does not mean that abusers should ever feel okay about their sexually abusive behavior. It just means that if abusers can feel only shame, a strong part of their cycle for doing the abuse still exists. Abusers need to do everything they can to start changing not only how they see others but also how they see themselves. To be safe, abusers need to have increased self-esteem and an increased belief in the skills they have learned to control their behavior.

Perhaps the abuser has apologized and promised never to sexually abuse again. Even if he or she could keep that promise, would that be enough? Are an apology and a promise enough in other situations in which someone has caused damage? It is often difficult to directly confront *anyone* with issues that bother us. It is even harder to confront someone with whom we have a personal relationship. The fear of losing that relationship can keep us silent about our true feelings. Rather than deal with an issue, we minimize or ignore the problem. In the next story, we see why sometimes we go on as if nothing has happened, even when someone has hurt us. It illustrates the mental struggle between wanting and not wanting to recognize the harm that friends and family can cause.

The Broken Porch Post

One quiet evening you are sitting in your home watching television when suddenly there's a loud crash and the whole house shakes, shattering your peace. Startled and frightened, you run to the front door only to discover your neighbor's car has crashed into the corner of your porch. The roof is sagging down almost touching the car.

Speechless, you watch your neighbor slowly emerge unharmed from the car. He looks up, somewhat dazed, and says sadly, "Would you just look at that corner post. Gee, am I ever sorry. I did it. I'm the one responsible for it. I am the driver and I should have known better."

He gets back in his car, starts to back away, then leans out the window to add, "Oh say, I've been meaning to tell you for some time now. You know, you really did build this house way too close to the road. You might want to think about setting it back before someone really gets hurt. But I am sorry. I promise it won't happen again. I know myself. You've got my word."

Would that be enough of an apology? He acknowledged damaging the post, but what about the porch roof, the destroyed shrubs, the new rose bush from Mother's Day, the perennial plants you've been nurturing for years, the torn-up lawn, your child's mangled tricycle?

Was the apology enough, or would you expect him to repair the damage? Wouldn't you want to know how it happened? Did he fall asleep at the wheel? Was drinking involved? If so, wouldn't you want him to go for treatment? Wouldn't you want some reassurance that it wouldn't happen again? Is his promise enough to make you feel comfortable letting your child ride her tricycle in the driveway again?

The shock has worn off, and now you are absolutely furious. How dare he do this to your home and your peace of mind! You begin remembering all the times your neighbor has been distracted at the wheel while talking on his cell phone or playing with the radio or reaching into a bag for coffee and donuts. You remember the way he always drives too fast in the neighborhood, even when kids are outside playing. You wonder why you've never said anything to him before.

Then gradually you recall what a good friend he has been. He gives you a ride to work every day so you can leave the car for your wife. He offers you the use of his lawn mower when yours is broken. He even spent a Saturday fixing your bathroom faucets because he knew you didn't have money for a plumber. And his wife watches your kids every day after school until you get home from work.

You think to yourself, "Why, this guy would give me the shirt off his back. How often do friends like this come along, anyway? After all, it's only a porch post. It probably won't cost that much to fix it myself."

This story is another metaphor — a story that's similar to a child abuse situation, even though it's not exactly the same. The damage that a car crashing into a porch post can cause is nothing like the potential harm that sexual abuse can cause a child. But the personal reactions to the upsetting event in the story are like the reactions that many family members and friends have to learning about the sexual abuse of a child. The careless neighbor–porch post story allows you to imagine yourself in a situation where you can understand many of the factors that influence the way people respond to difficult circumstances.

Sometimes, when we are outside a particular situation it is easier to think clearly about how people in those situations should react. In cases of child sexual abuse, we might think that a child should be able to tell, or we might think that a nonabusing parent should be able to confront the abuser. But we can see from this story that many factors—friendship, affection, gratitude, dependence on the wrongdoer—can cause people to have many different reactions (including shock, disbelief, anger, confusion, self-doubt, minimizing thoughts, denial, or even "forgiveness") when negative events occur. Forgiveness is a particularly confusing reaction if it comes before the wrongdoer (or abuser) has taken responsibility and worked hard to repair the harm done.[4]

Perhaps this metaphor helps you understand how difficult it is even for *adults* to sort through their confused feelings and confront another adult friend on whom they depend for help. Imagine for a moment how much more difficult, even frightening, it could be for nonabusing parents to sort through their confusion about what is going on and confront adult abusers on whom they depend for almost *everything* in their lives.

Imagine how much more confused a *child* might feel. Imagine how much more difficult, even frightening, it could be for a child to say no to secret sexual touching or to tell about the wrongdoing of a family member. The child's fear of telling can be even greater when the sexual abuser is someone he or she cares about, perhaps someone the whole family cares about. The confusion and fear can be especially great when the abusing person is a bigger adult or an older child, and when the abusing person is someone the victim depends on for daily love and care.

Notes

1. Peters, J. M. (1989). The wrong stuff. In J. Hindman, *Just before dawn* (pp. 25–34). Ontario, Ore.: AlexAndria Associates.

2. Hindman, J. (1989). *Just before dawn.* Ontario, Ore.: AlexAndria Associates.

3. Madanes, C. (1995). Training seminar on interventions in abusive relationships. February 10–14, 1995. Miami, Fla.

4. Hindman, J. (1989). *Just before dawn.* Ontario, Ore.: AlexAndria Associates.

IO

···

Child Sexual Abuse Is More than a Family Problem: It's a Crime

Child sexual abuse should always be treated as a crime. When abuse is done *to* or *by* a member of your family, however, it's natural for you to wish that it could be handled privately, like other family problems. Because families in which abuse occurs have to work with people outside the family, it is important to understand why child sexual abuse is not like any other family problem. If you can look at sexual abuse by a family member as a crime, just as you do when a stranger sexually abuses a child, you take seriously what has happened to the child and hold the abuser responsible for the harm.

Child sexual abuse is a crime because it violates children and families and steals from them, often without their awareness, just as a burglar steals from others when they are not looking. In her book *Just Before Dawn* (1989), Jan Hindman writes of the many ways abusers steal from and cause harm, or trauma, to abused children and to their families. Let's look at some of the ways abusers steal.

What the Abuser Steals from the Abused Child

Child sexual abusers steal children's *sense of safety* in their own family. Abusers steal other family members' natural *right to have trusting relationships* with one another. When an adult parent abuses a child and tricks that child into keeping a secret from the nonabusing parent, this abuser steals from the child the *right to have a close, honest, protective relationship with that nonabusing parent*. Family members should be able to trust one another, look out for one another, and protect one another.

By forcing sexual behaviors on children, abusers steal children's opportunity to choose their first partners and to experience sexual development naturally as they grow and mature. Abusers steal the special privacy of a child's body and the special choices that every individual, adult or child, should have about sex.

Children who are tricked into hiding things about themselves can develop a sense of shame and guilt. When they are tricked into hiding sexual touching, children may develop a sense of shame and guilt about all sexual behaviors. This association between sex and shame, if not repaired, may stay with children throughout life and affect the way they see themselves as adults in sexual relationships. Thus, abusers steal children's right to grow up with normal, healthy feelings about their own sexuality and may disturb their right as adults to experience joy in normal, healthy sexual relationships.

Abusers can steal children's self-esteem and their pride and confidence in themselves and how they live their lives. Abusers steal the carefree days that are supposed to be part of childhood. Sometimes the sexual abuse affects the child so much that the child is unable to perform in school or in nonacademic activities such as athletics, music, and various clubs. We have already looked at one of the most serious forms of injury that abused children and siblings may experience: faulty "radar," which can leave children unable to protect themselves in the outside world.

What the Abuser Steals from the Abused Child's Siblings

All children in a family, brothers and sisters as well as abused children, may experience similar kinds of injury and lose similar kinds of rights when sexual abuse happens in their family, even though their experiences are not the same. Sexually abused children experience a direct violation to their own bodies and to their minds whenever the abuser sexually touches them or requires them to sexually touch the abuser, to witness sexual acts, or to perform sexual acts on others. Children may experience sexual abuse in a deep and profound way. Whenever siblings live in the same family environment under the same abuser's web of secrecy, manipulation, and control, siblings too are likely to experience a loss of their emotional and psychological well-being.

In some situations, siblings have no direct way of knowing about the abuse. Sometimes, however, the brothers and sisters "kind of" know that something bad is going on. Sometimes they do not know exactly what the problem is. Other times, they know exactly what is going on. Sometimes they even see or hear the abuse. Sometimes they hear the abused child cry out. To varying degrees, these aware siblings may experience trauma by *bearing witness* to the trauma of others. This is called indirect or *vicarious* trauma. It is the type of trauma many people experience when watching any kind of violence or abuse to others in reality, on television, or in the theater. You can probably think of many television programs or movies that are upsetting for adults and inappropriate for children.

Many times the abuser has also directly sexually abused the siblings, but these children are too frightened to tell. They may be particularly frightened if they have already seen how much pain the family is experiencing because of one disclosure. Siblings may hold back their information because they do not want to add to the family's emotional pain and because they don't want to receive the same family anger that may have been directed toward the abused child following disclosure. Most of the time, siblings feel powerless to do anything. Siblings in families where abuse occurs have to find ways to tolerate an *intolerable* situation. Thus, all children in the family may, to varying degrees, suffer similar hidden injuries and emotional pain.

It may be hard to think of siblings as being hurt if they do not report any direct sexual touch by the abuser. Let's think, though, about how brothers and sisters of sexually abused children learn about the world, about sex, about privacy of the body, about trust and honesty, about relationships, about how to use their own "radar" to tell the difference between risk and safety. If siblings' first awareness of sexual behavior is through exposure to a sexually abusive relationship, say between a father and a sister, then siblings may experience a *disturbance in their own thoughts and feelings about sex and about relationships.* They may indirectly learn that allowing themselves to be used in a sexual way is the way to get attention and affection. *Their own normal sexual development and development of intimate relationships may become distorted.*

Siblings can struggle between being aware and not wanting to be aware. They can wear "blinders" and learn to shut off their "radar," so they do not have to deal with a problem that is out of their control. If siblings develop faulty radar and can't be sure that sexual touching between a parent and their brother or sister is wrong, how can they be sure that sexual touching is wrong with a teacher or with a camp counselor?

When the abuser manipulates siblings to keep the secret, these children can have *their sense of safety in the home* stolen from them. They may live with *ongoing fear* that discovery of the abuse will lead to the end of the family. If the nonabusing parent seems unaware of the abuse, both the directly abused child and the siblings may become disrespectful and distrusting of that nonabusing parent. Thus, the abuser also can *distort and hurt the children's relationship with the nonabusing parent,* as the children no longer see that parent as someone to whom they can go with their worries.

When siblings see the abuser give more "special" time and attention to one child, they may have feelings of *rejection and low self-esteem,* as well as *resentment toward the child who is being abused.* As these feelings build, siblings may *lose their ability to have a positive relationship with the abused child.* And after disclosure, if siblings become confused about who is responsible, they might feel further anger and resentment, not toward the abuser who *caused* the problem but toward the abused child for *revealing* the problem.

The accompanying chart shows some of the ways that sexual abuse in a family can hurt children. Not all abused children and siblings experience trauma in all these areas. A complete assessment by professionals is necessary to find out all the types of trauma.

What the Abuser Steals from the Parent, Guardian, or Spouse

Although the relationships are different, adult and adolescent abusers can hurt nonabusing parents in similar ways. Abusers steal from nonabusing parents the *natural pride* they have in knowing that they have been able to

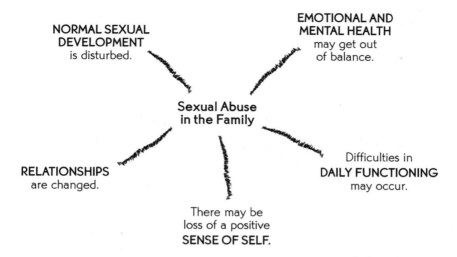

NORMAL SEXUAL
DEVELOPMENT
is disturbed.

EMOTIONAL AND
MENTAL HEALTH
may get out
of balance.

Sexual Abuse
in the Family

RELATIONSHIPS
are changed.

Difficulties in
DAILY FUNCTIONING
may occur.

There may be
loss of a positive
SENSE OF SELF.

provide their child with *a safe home* where the child can learn to distinguish right from wrong, healthy sexuality from abusive sexuality, honesty from dishonesty.

Nonabusing parents or guardians experience emotional pain as they live with the losses associated with the abuse of their children: *peace of mind* is replaced by rage that their child has been violated. It's the parents' job to lose sleep and experience stress when their children are sick or injured or having serious problems, but no parents should have to spend years after disclosure *worrying about the potential impact of sexual abuse* on their children.

Adults in a family, the nonabusing parents and guardians of children, have *their sense of well-being and their sense of themselves* stolen. Nonabusing parents experience other types of losses, depending on whether the abuser is an adult partner or an adolescent or older child of the nonabusing parent.

When the abuser is both the adult partner of the nonabusing parent and the parent or stepparent or parent figure of the abused child, nonabusing parents usually experience an extreme sense of personal loss. The sexually abusing adult steals the nonabusing parent's *right to have a faithful and trusted partner* with whom to share an intimate, caring relationship and to share parenting of the children. Even when adults are divorced, they should be able to share parenting in a trusting relationship. No parents should have to worry that their partner or any adult could turn to their children for sexual activity. By requiring children to keep the sexual touching a secret from the nonabusing parent, adult abusers steal the nonabusing parent's *right to have a totally close, honest, open relationship with all the children.*

When the abuser is an adolescent child, he or she steals from his or her parents the *natural pride* parents have when their children behave in positive ways. The adolescent abuser also steals from the abused child's parents the *right to trust their younger children in the care of older children* for short periods of time. No parents should have to be afraid that sexual activity could occur if they leave their younger children in the care of their own adolescent children or in the care of adolescent babysitters.

When both the abusing and the abused children are in the same family, the losses are magnified. The nonabusing parents are often divided in their feelings for each child, alternating between blaming and feeling sympathy for the abusing child or blaming and feeling empathy for the child who was abused. Because these parents care about both children, they often do not allow themselves to feel the full rage about what happened to their abused child. As a result, children abused by a sibling frequently do not experience their parents' full support.

What the Abuser Steals from the Family

While child sexual abusers in the family steal from individuals, they also steal from the family as a whole. If the family "secret" about the abuser in your family was revealed in school or in the community, you may have felt a loss of pride in your family and experienced *shame* and *embarrassment*. If you are an abused child, or a brother or sister or cousin of an abused child or an abuser, you might have had a hard time even going to school. If you are the nonabusing parent, you might have had a hard time going to the supermarket or to school meetings or to work, where everyone seems to know about your family's problem. Thus, abusers *steal a family's pride in its identity as a "regular" family.* You may have developed a perception of yourselves as an "incest" family. It may seem at times as if the heart or the spirit has gone out of your family. The abuser in your situation has taken away your right to have a happy, safe family atmosphere where you can enjoy one another without worrying about abuse. The abuser has taken away your family's sense of the world as a safe place. If, as parents, you cannot trust that your children are safe in your own home, how will you be able to trust that your children are safe in the community?

Sometimes, members of an extended family may end up "taking sides" when an incest disclosure is made. When that happens, a family may lose the support of cousins, aunts, uncles, grandparents, or others. Often the abused or abusing child's family feels shunned by neighbors and friends who understandably are fearful of letting their children play at a home where sexual abuse has occurred. Sometimes a family finds it easier to move and start over in a new neighborhood. In these situations, the abuser's behavior has caused the family to lose their home, neighborhood, school, and friends.

What the Abuser Loses

Though it is not part of any legal or criminal assessment, it is important in a therapeutic trauma assessment to note that child sexual abusers also steal from and cause harm to themselves. They steal their own ability to feel pride, self-esteem, a sense of accomplishment in something good. They adopt an unhealthy view of sexuality, perhaps fueling that view with distorted or pornographic sexual material. They disturb their own ability to develop a healthy sexual identity by using a child as an object for their own pleasure. They can become focused on patterns of sexual arousal that are forbidden in our culture, by their religion, or by our laws. Left untreated, these may become lifelong patterns in adolescents who are in the early stages of developing their sexuality and their ability to be intimate with others. Adolescent abusers give up the choice to keep sexual experiences within peer relationships. And above all, as you may know from your own situation, adolescent abusers rob themselves of a life of being trusted by their family members.

II

Assessment of Trauma and Other Injuries: Why the Whole Family Can't Be Together for a While

We've looked at many parts of sexually abusive behavior and many hidden or disguised ways that children and other family members can be hurt by sexual abuse. In Part Four we will look at how specialized treatment can be helpful to each person in the family. There are some parts of treatment that are the same for all abusers, and some parts that are the same for all abused children, but treatment does not look exactly the same for everyone. No two people and no two families are alike.

Treatment is planned around understanding the needs of each individual and each family. To develop that understanding with your family, therapists will do an *assessment* to learn how sexual abuse has affected each of you, and in what areas your family wants or needs help coping with feelings, thoughts, and behaviors, and to determine what changes will help everyone move forward in life. The assessment period is a very important time for clients and therapists to work together to gather as much information as possible and to plan treatment goals that make a difference.

The assessment is a getting-to-know-you process that looks different for each person in the family. There is one thing that all assessments look for: how does each person in the family understand and feel about the sexual abuse and the people involved? With nonabusing parents, the goal is to understand what, if anything, each parent needs to change to feel confident in his or her ability to protect the children in the future. With abused children and their siblings, the assessment focus is not just on learning how the child has been harmed and the level of trauma but also on making sure that the child is aware of all the ways he or she continues to be wonderful and lovable. What is being evaluated is *not* what's wrong with a child but what each child needs to ease the pain and to feel safe in his or her family.

Unfortunately, there's no easy way to sit with the emotional pain that may come up as you and other family members work to uncover and discover the facts around the who, what, when, where, and how of what happened. But if you can learn to tolerate hearing about and thinking about all the painful facts and feelings, chances are good that you'll be able to talk about and listen to facts about painful situations in the future, including whether abuse is occurring.

And there's no quick fix for sexually abusive behavior. With abusers, besides uncovering the facts, the assessment goal is to determine whether the abuser has the courage to take responsibility for the abuse and the commitment to work hard to change old ways and to learn new ways to prevent abusing behavior in the future. Often the assessing therapist will be looking at things like level of cooperation, consistency in getting to treatment and paying the bill (adults), capacity to be totally honest, ability to abide by rules of treatment and of safety in the community, and a sincere determination to choose another way of life that doesn't involve abusing others.

During treatment, the abuser will learn to understand that his or her behavior occurs in patterns (cycles), learn to recognize how his or her beliefs and thoughts are distorted and manipulative (thinking errors), develop a plan to prevent a return to abusive behavior (relapse prevention plan), and set up a strong support and supervision system of people (including family members, probation or parole officers, social workers, religious leaders, Alcoholics or Narcotics Anonymous meetings and sponsors, and neighbors and friends, when appropriate) who will help him or her not abuse in the future. It is important that the abuser has people around to discuss feelings, potential risk situations for relapse, and positive coping strategies.

During the investigation and in the early stages of treatment, an adult or older adolescent abuser is usually required to live away from the home where the abused child or other younger children live. This separation allows the family to use the emotional and physical space to think about what happened during the abuse and to participate in the assessment.

It is important to uncover all the information needed, so that everyone can understand the problem of sexual abuse in the family as completely as possible. Only then can the treatment providers and the family work together to design a treatment plan based not only on the facts but also on some of the feelings, thoughts, and family patterns in relationships. This is similar to the way you would deal with other injuries, such as damage to your property. In most situations, although people often want things to go back to normal as quickly as possible, they first want to investigate just how much harm has been done.

Say, for example, you are on a long car trip and something unexpectedly goes wrong with the car, causing you to be in an accident. There appears to be a lot of damage. Would you just take the car to the body shop and have the fender fixed? Newly painted, the car would look normal from the outside. But before piling everyone back in to continue on the journey, wouldn't you want to make sure that the car is safe and unlikely to crash again? Wouldn't you have the mechanics check for damage to the frame, to the engine, to the steering and brakes? Wouldn't you want to know if the driver had ignored any signals or warning lights on the dashboard that there were problems, or even hid the problems from the rest of the family just because the driver was so determined to get to a certain place? You might want to change drivers, or even teach others how to drive. You might teach all the passengers what noises to listen for so that everyone can tell when something is wrong. And above all, you would want to teach the passengers how to signal for help when it is needed.

This metaphor of the car accident has some similarities to sexual abuse situations. Just like the car seemed to be going along just fine before the accident, life in your family seemed to be going along just fine before the awareness of sexual abuse created the feelings of a family "crash." The "journey" of life is interrupted in both situations. In the car accident situation, the passengers could look for help in many forms: perhaps first a tow truck, then the insurance agent, then a mechanic, and, finally, experts in the body shop. In sexual abuse situations, family members also can look for help in many forms: schoolteachers or guidance counselors, other family members, friends, church members, protective services workers, foster parents, medical professionals, lawyers and judges, and specially trained therapists.

Think of the work investigators put into learning what caused the crash of an airplane that looked perfectly normal. Families of the crash victims demand to know the truth, to know who or what was responsible. They often wait anxiously for months and months while the investigation of the crash goes on. Authorities sometimes try to reassemble all the shattered pieces of the plane as they search for clues. They want to make sure they understand why this plane crashed, so they can fix any problems in the design of the airplane, the maintenance procedures, or pilot training and try to prevent any crashes in the future.

It is the same idea when treating sexual abuse in a family. Before the disclosure or discovery of sexual abuse, from a distance, it might have looked like everything was "normal." In reality, there were problems beneath the surface of your family's life, and the disclosure lifted the protective cover of secrecy. The next step is to find all the pieces of information you can: all the manipulative patterns, all the facts about the abusive behavior, all the pieces of the family's problem. Then you can understand why — in addition to "pilot error" — your family "crashed." Then you can figure out what went wrong and what needs to be fixed before deciding whether it's safe to live together again. The purpose of treatment for abused children and other family members is to help them deal with the pain of facing the truth, to understand what happened, to heal from any emotional and psychological wounds, and to prevent abuse from ever occurring again.

The purpose of treatment is not to punish abusers. That is the job of the courts: to decide punishment, including the possibility of a prison sentence. Most courts order specific sexual abuser treatment, either in prison or during a long period of probation or parole. Specialized treatment offers to teach sexual abusers mental, emotional, and behavioral skills to help repair the emotional pain and harm their abuse caused the abused children and their family members, and to build a sense of pride through learning to be in control of their own behavior and their own lives. The first step for abusers in rebuilding their self-esteem and pride is to be honest about what they have done and to take full responsibility for the abuse. Abusers must work *hard in treatment* to understand *where inside themselves* their behavior came from and how to prevent themselves from ever abusing again.

An especially important part of building pride in oneself is developing *empathy*, the capacity to care for others, to understand how others feel, and to be able to put the needs of others before one's own needs or desires. Without empathy, there is no way to care about the harm done to others, and thus no way to prevent returning to abusive behavior. Once abusers are able to empathize with their abused children and with other family members, they can begin the long process of trying to repair the pain and harm they have caused others.

"What steps led me to abuse?" and "How did I do it?" are two big questions abusers need to answer before asking the more important question, "*How will I stop myself from ever doing it again?*" It is not just the abusers' questions about themselves, however, that must be answered. It is important for everyone else in the family to understand how the abuser tricked and hurt them and what made them respond to the abuse situation the way they did. Some of the questions you might be asking yourself right now are, "Why didn't or couldn't I protect my child?" or "Why didn't I help?" or "Why didn't I tell?" or even, "Why didn't I know?" The answers to these questions will help determine in what ways others in the family also need to make changes.

12

....

When Supervised Visitation Makes Sense

When the abuser is someone outside the family, you might clearly understand why the abuser should be kept away from all children, but especially from the children he or she abused. But when the abuser is someone you care about, someone who has been part of your life for years, you are more likely to be confused. You may feel torn between not trusting the abuser and missing him or her. Sometimes you may want to think that the abuse is a smaller problem than it really is. The abuser may also miss being part of the family and want to think of the abusive behavior as being less serious or partly someone else's responsibility. Sometimes the child who has been abused also misses the abuser and wants to think of the abuse as being less serious than it really is.

Perhaps you understand why the abuser, the abused child, and the family need treatment. You may understand why it is *not* a good idea for the family to live with an abuser who is in the early stages of assessment and treatment. But still you want some regular visits to keep the family members connected. The children, even the abused child, may be pleading to see the abuser again. A treatment program that is focused on the needs of the children will assess first whether any contact is in the child's best interest and then whether the abuser is ready for contact in therapy sessions. When everyone is ready, contact during therapy can focus on repairing relationships that have been betrayed.

One of the most frequently asked questions in the *early* stages of disclosure and treatment is, "Why can't abusers have contact *outside* of therapy sessions with the children they didn't touch? Why can't we at least have a Sunday visit together?" This is a good question coming from the heart of a family that has been divided. No one wants children to suffer anymore than they have already. The answer to this question is very complicated, with many parts.

There are important factors behind the decision to control contact with someone who has sexually abused a child.[1] First, it is not a good idea to let someone who has this behavior problem be near *any* children — at least not before it is clear how severe the problem is or whether the abuser is treatable and able to learn how to control the problem. It doesn't make sense to give an abuser the privilege of being with children until that person has become involved in and begun to make progress in treatment. If the sexual abuser was a person outside the family, such as a teacher or scout leader, no one would say, "The abuse only happened with Billy. Let's let the teacher or leader still work with the other children." In fact, most people would be furious if a school hired a teacher with any history of sexually abusing children. Most people would not want to worry every day whether their children were safe.

What harm could it do, you might ask, as long as someone supervises the children's visits with the abuser? That is a good question, especially when the child who was victimized wants to see the abuser. The child's strong bond of love and trust with the abuser is often the main reason the person was able to abuse the child. The child should be allowed to see the abuser if he or she wants to, *but not before it is emotionally safe for the child to do so.* Before they are allowed to be with children, abusers have to work hard in specialized treatment to become honest about their problem and to identify the ways they emotionally and mentally manipulated the child and other members of the family. They must admit their responsibility for the abuse to the abused children and to the rest of the family during therapy sessions.

Specially trained treatment providers and protective services workers are taught to determine the nature of the abuser's problem and whether he or she has come far enough in treatment to have contact with the abused child. Because it usually takes a long time for abusers to learn all about their problem, it also takes a long time for the nonabusing parent or caretaker to learn all this information.

Understanding the abuser's behavior is necessary for *anyone* who is going to supervise visitation, whether that person is a family member or not. Otherwise, the visit supervisor might not recognize the abuser's manipulative techniques. During a visit with the abused child or any other children, the abuser could once again use these hidden techniques to gain control. Imagine the effect on the victim, for example, when he or she looks into the sad eyes of the abuser, who has been living apart from the family. During the abuse, the child may have learned that the way to win love was to please the abuser. This child might want to protect and please the abuser, or even please the family, by taking back everything that was said in the disclosure, or recanting. Visits planned too early in treatment, therefore, can confuse the situation more.

It may seem unfair to keep brothers and sisters of abused children from having contact with an abuser, especially if that abuser plays an important role in their lives. In some ways, it is not fair. It is sad for all the children involved, but let's think of the bigger picture. It wouldn't be fair to the siblings who have not reported any abuse to let them think that they would be safe around the untreated abuser, and that only the victim could be abused. As noted earlier, abusers may have more than one victim in a family. If the abuser has also abused a sibling who has not yet told anyone, visits with the abuser might increase the pressure on the sibling *not* to tell. During visits, an abused sibling of the child who already disclosed abuse may act as if everything is okay because he or she doesn't want to be left out of the family, as the abused child already is. A nonabusing parent, seeing the family appear to be happy together, might begin to see the problem as less serious, as something that happened only between the abuser and one specific child. As a result, the abused child would *continue* to pay a big emotional price for the abuse, while the abuser would keep on receiving the family's emotional support. Siblings who may have been pushed aside during the abuse might have a hard time resisting the extra attention the abuser would now give them during visits. In addition, the abuser, already feeling lonely and afraid of losing his or her family, might act as if he or she was not risky to be around. The abuser might look extra lovable, or perhaps extra lonely, during those visits, not to mention trying very hard to be on his or her best behavior.

It wouldn't be fair to have family visits without the victimized child. Being left out of visits could feel like punishment to a child. Excluding the abused child during these visits would make sense only if it was something about the abused child that caused the abuser to abuse. That is *not* true. *Abusers are the ones who have the problem controlling their own behavior.* Since we already know that they have not been able to keep from touching at least one child, we must be sure that they learn how to keep themselves from manipulating and touching any child.

Besides, if everyone except the abused child was able to see the abuser, the family members might have to act as if they "forgot" about the abuse while they were visiting with the abuser. In order to gain the abuser's love or even to help him or her feel better, the abused child's brothers and sisters may push away thoughts and feelings about what happened to the abused child. In order not to feel bad about leaving the abused child out, the siblings might even start to blame the child who was abused for all the trouble in the family. The children might say something like, "If it weren't for *her*, that little pain, we could be together like we used to be." Or they might say, "We don't need *him* in this family — we're better off without that little troublemaker." Even when the abused child does *not* want to be around the abuser, the other children might blame the abused child because *they* can't see the abuser.

Siblings who have also been abused but have not disclosed often have mixed feelings. They may feel relief that someone else told so the abuse would stop, or they may blame the disclosing child for taking the special attention of the abuser away or for ruining the family: "If I didn't have to tell, why did she? It was no big deal anyway."

These kinds of feelings set up the abused child as the scapegoat, the one who gets blamed for breaking up the family. Reactions like these not only cause more confusion in the family; they also cause family members to feel more divided and the family to feel torn apart. This confusion of feelings can make it difficult for family members in treatment to do the hard work of figuring out the *what*, the *how*, and the *why* of the sexual abuse. This confusion makes it more difficult for the abusers to be honest, to understand their behavior, to repair emotional and psychological harm, and to learn ways to control their own behavior.

Abusers' own shame about their abusive behavior makes it difficult to face the truth. The confusion also makes it harder for abused children and other family members to deal with their own feelings or their roles in the web of secrecy.

If the family is to become a safe place for children, *all* family members must understand that the *abuser* is the one responsible for the turmoil and for his or her absence from the family. It is because abusers do not control themselves that children are used and harmed in the first place. It is because abusers harm children that they have to keep themselves separate from their victims and from the families.

It is because abusers make homes unsafe that they should move out. It is not enough to admit the problem, to promise not to do it again, and then get back together. The abuser's behavior has wounded the family emotionally and psychologically — and often financially — and caused an "infection" in the family spirit. Just as in treating any infection that could spread through the body, the wound must be cleaned out before covering it with bandages.

Let's look at another kind of wound that almost everyone has experienced and understands how to treat. Think of it like this. You get a splinter deep inside your finger. On the outside, from a distance, you can't see the splinter. But you know it's there, it's irritating, and you can feel the discomfort.

Would you leave it there? It looks normal from the outside. But you know the splinter has to come out, even though getting a splinter out can be painful. Sometimes you have to soak it for a long time or use special tools, such as a sterilized needle or some sharp tweezers and a magnifying glass.

Sometimes you get most of it, but it does not come out in one piece. It still hurts, so you know a piece of the splinter is still in there. Now, you may have to make a small cut to open up the wound so you can reach the splinter with tweezers. You have to hold the cut open so you can clean the wound. Why make such a big fuss over a tiny splinter, over the tiniest piece that's left in your finger? Because you know that if you do not get out every bit, you could get an infection, and the condition could get worse.

Treatment of sexual abuse in a family is very complicated, but in some ways it is similar to removing a splinter. Sometimes the large, visible parts of the problem are removed fairly quickly: the abuser may have admitted the problem and promised never to do it again. To outsiders, the family might look like everything is back to "normal," as the children continue in school, participating in their sports or clubs or music lessons.

But remember that family members who have lived in abusive situations often learn to look good on the outside, even when they are unhappy or angry or afraid on the inside. Even when family members don't know about the abuse (their "splinter"), they usually know that things don't feel right in the family. They can often feel the unhappiness in the family but can't figure out exactly where it is coming from.

Just as a splinter can cause infection in the body, so the hidden parts of an abuse problem can continue to infect the heart of the whole family. This means that all family members must learn to bear the emotional pain of being separated from the abuser until the abuse, the problem that has wounded the family, has been cleaned out and true healing can begin. This is no easy task, but there really is no choice. So it is up to the abusers to understand everything they can about how they developed the problem and how they can stop their abusive behavior.

In the beginning, the abuser should not be in contact with children outside of counseling sessions. When the abuser is allowed to visit with the children too soon, it can slow treatment and make it less effective. The patterns that let the abuse happen in the first place can be rebuilt very quickly. Children are not safe in families where abusers have not learned whether and how they can control their behavior. Children are not safe in families where nonabusing adults do not understand the abuser's behavior and their own responses to the abuser. Children are not safe in families unless nonabusing parents have the courage to look within themselves to determine whether there are areas that need to change so that they are in a strong position in the family. Children are not emotionally safe in families who can't protect them from abuse.

Note

1. Meinig, M. B., & Bonner, B. L. (1990). Returning the treated sex offender to the family. *Violence Update, 1*, 1–11.

part three

Longer Stories About Secret Behavior in the Family

13

"Stealing the Family Cookies": A Story of Adult Manipulation

We have been looking at the different thoughts, feelings, and behaviors related to sexual abuse. We have been looking at ways to understand the kinds of hidden, "invisible" harm that sexual abuse can cause, whether from exhibitionism or fondling or intercourse. The abuse could have happened a few times or over a long period of time. Hidden emotional and psychological pain happens frequently in all kinds of abuse, and it is rare that there is no damage at all.

The longer stories—metaphors—in this chapter and the next put all these elements together to show the actual harm that occurs within a family when one person has the power to manipulate and control others. The stories show that although the physical act done to the child is the crime, it is the carefully woven web of secret manipulation that causes the hidden psychological and emotional harm to individuals and to family relationships.

This invisible harm can occur whether the manipulation involves sexual abuse or nonsexual behavior. The stories that follow are not about sexual abuse, but they are about abuse of power in family relationships. "Stealing the Family Cookies" will be most helpful if the abuser in your family was a parent or stepparent or some other adult. Chapter 14, "Borrowing the Family Car," will be more helpful if the abuser in your family was an older child or adolescent. Neither of these stories will be exactly like your story, but they will help you recognize some behaviors and patterns within your family. On the surface, the stories might seem exaggerated or even far-fetched. Read the stories in the way you might read a fairy tale or Aesop's fables or any other obviously fictional story. You will find something in the story to help you understand how manipulations control family members and cause emotional, mental, and relationship problems. Notice that what happens in these stories also happens in families where sexual abuse occurs.

> *Read this story with an eye toward discovering hidden signs of injury, manipulative patterns, and the roles that each family member plays in a situation in which an adult is able to abuse power and authority.*

> *(If the abuser in your family is not an adult, you might want to skip this story for now and go straight to the story in Chapter 14, "Borrowing the Family Car.")*

Stealing the Family Cookies

One Sunday afternoon, Gail works for hours, baking hundreds of cookies for a family reunion the following weekend. A hardworking woman with a full-time job, she has one goal for the afternoon: to get all the cookie baking done for the family reunion next Saturday. Gail does not want to worry about getting it done during the week. She has been standing on her feet for hours, and she is tired and a little irritated that the kids are cluttering up the kitchen and asking for her attention. She sends 6-year-old Pete Junior — they call him PJ — and 8-year-old Susie outside to play, while telling 14-year-old Tara that she has no time to help with her homework. She tells her husband, Pete, that he will have to fix his own lunch today.

Pete also works hard — he holds down two jobs trying to provide for his family. He doesn't have much free time to spend with either the children or Gail, or even just to relax. He feels upset that Gail is not putting him first and taking care of his needs. Finally, around 4:30, Gail has finished her baking and is pleased with her work. She is relieved to be done.

The house has been full of delicious baking smells all day. Gail can see the hungry looks in her family's eyes. "Now don't touch a single one of these cookies," Gail explains. "I don't want to show up at the reunion without my full contribution. You can have some then, but for now you'll just have to wait. Besides, they are all arranged just so, and it would ruin the arrangement to take even one.

"Now, I know I can trust you two," she says to Tara and Pete. "I'll put them up on top of the refrigerator so Susie and PJ won't get at them." Exhausted, she announces that she is going to rest a bit before she fixes supper. She sighs and goes off to the bedroom.

Sitting at the kitchen table, Pete looks up at the cookies, smiles, and nudges his daughter, Tara, who has been busy doing her homework. "Hey, would you just look at that enormous pile of cookies — there must be hundreds of them up there. Your mother sure worked hard. But she sure does make a big deal out of things. I mean, imagine that a couple of missing cookies would really make a difference.

"You'd think she was talking about something really valuable, for goodness sake. Give me a break! It's not like they're gold out of Fort Knox. You know, Tara, she has really lost it this time. She has her values all twisted around. I mean, they're only cookies. Jeez, Mom couldn't even fix my lunch or give you the help you needed with your homework. And how long are the other kids supposed to play outside?

"I tell you, it's just not right to make us smell all these delicious smells, push us aside, and not even give us a single cookie. I mean, I worked hard all week to provide for this family. Why, I even paid for the ingredi-ents for the cookies, if you want to know the truth. I think I am entitled to a little appreciation at the end of the week, 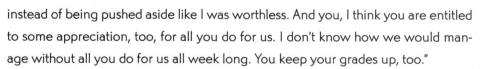 instead of being pushed aside like I was worthless. And you, I think you are entitled to some appreciation, too, for all you do for us. I don't know how we would man-age without all you do for us all week long. You keep your grades up, too."

Tara has been growing increasingly uncomfortable while her father speaks. Then Pete puts his arm around her and says, "Hey, Tara, what do you say? Let's each take just one. We can take two cookies from the back of the plate and nobody will even notice. She'll never even miss them. Besides, your mother never knows about much of anything, never mind what is going on around here."

Now, Tara is even more uncomfortable and anxious. "I don't think so, Dad. Mom baked those cookies, and she expects us to leave them alone. I wouldn't feel right."

Pete tightens his hug, winks, and says, more playfully, "Oh, come on, honey. You're my girl, we're together in this, aren't we? I know your Mom works hard. Why, I wouldn't even think of suggesting this if I thought it was really wrong. She is just overtired. Why, I bet she even expects us to cheat just a little. I mean, don't all families snitch from the cookie jar? I wouldn't do it if it were really wrong, now would I? I'm your Dad."

Tara is more and more anxious, confused by her mixed-up thoughts and feelings. Dad hardly ever spends any time with her, but now he's confiding in her, telling her his feelings. She feels special, close to him. She wishes he would spend more time with her, be affectionate more often.

"But," she thinks to herself, "Mom works so hard, too. She usually has time to help me or to take me places. Just yesterday she took me to the mall to get running shoes. She even took me to lunch for a special time together. There's going to be a ton of people at the reunion. I know that if she had enough ingredients to bake extra cookies, she would have given us all some. But I heard her say she ran out of flour and sugar. I know she appreciates me and trusts me. It wouldn't be right to take those cookies. I wouldn't be able to look her in the eye.

"But then look at Dad—he looks so tired and sad. He does work hard. Mom should pay more attention to him. It is kind of silly, even mean not to let him have a stupid old cookie. I don't care much for myself. Sure, I like cookies, but I can wait until next weekend.

"But Dad needs something," Tara thinks, "not just the cookie, but a little special attention. I guess he's kind of counting on me. I know I like to feel special, too."

Pete is waiting for an answer. "Oh, I just don't know, Dad," she murmurs.

"Oh, come on," says Pete. "Just you and me."
Pete takes her hand and pulls her up from the
table and over to the refrigerator. They each
take a cookie from the back of the huge plate
and return to the table. Pete thoroughly enjoys
his cookie, but Tara's pleasure is ruined by guilt
over breaking her mother's trust. She is afraid of
how mad her mother will be when they get
caught.

A little later, Gail comes into the kitchen to
fix supper. She glances up at the plate of cookies and goes to the door to call the
younger children. "What did I tell you?" whispers Pete with a smile. "She never
even noticed. There's plenty left. And you must admit, it tasted great and *you* really
enjoyed it. I know you did. You were chewing so slowly, loving every moment.
You've got to admit, *we* pulled a fast one."

Tara smiles back at him, but her stomach is churning and her thoughts are
whirling: "I feel so ashamed. He's right. I did like the taste of the cookie. And it's not
like he forced me. I'm not a little kid. *My* hand reached for the cookie. I can't believe
Mom didn't notice, just like he said. I guess Dad really knows what's going on. He
must be right. Even if she had noticed, she probably wouldn't really have cared. It *is*
only a cookie. It's no big deal, just this once."

The next day Pete and Gail arrive home at the same time. Gail goes to change
clothes before fixing supper. Pete walks into the kitchen where Tara is doing her
homework at the table. Susie and PJ are outside playing. He gives her a hug and a
kiss on the forehead. "Boy, am I starving! Supper won't be ready for at least another hour, by the time your mother gets going on
it," he says, with disgust in his voice. "I think a little snack would be in order, don't you? How
about we grab another one of those cookies?"

Tara again feels the anxious churning in her
stomach. She feels torn between wanting to
please Dad but not wanting to go against Mom
by sneaking behind her back.

"Oh, I don't think so, Dad. I'm not too hungry yet."

Pete sits near her, again puts his arm around her, and coaxes, "Oh, come on. We're in it together now. What difference does it make if we take one or twenty cookies? If your mom is going to get mad, she'll be mad either way. Besides, I really don't think she would mind. If she was really concerned, wouldn't she inspect the plate just a bit more closely? I think so. Now, she's not going to come right out and give us permission, but she won't exactly check it out, either.

"I probably shouldn't tell you this, but your mother's kind of the nervous type, gets wrapped up in her own world. I mean, doesn't she know it's supper time? She should have a meal ready to go in the oven. Maybe her way of not feeling guilty is to leave those cookies where we can get at them. Besides, don't forget how good they tasted yesterday and what fun we had with our little secret. Come on, let's go, before your mother catches us." With that, Pete again brings her over to the refrigerator, where again they take the cookies.

Just then, PJ and Susie burst into the kitchen from outside. Pete is caught off guard. The children wonder what in the world is going on.

Before they can speak, Pete angrily yells out, "What are you kids doing in this kitchen with those muddy sneakers? Your mother works hard to keep this house clean. You are so thoughtless to track dirt all over the place. Go take those sneakers off outside. In fact, I don't want you to come into this house again without knocking on the door, so I can come and check your sneakers before you come in. Just look at that dirt! Why, I have a mind to punish you kids with no television tonight. I'll give you just one more chance to be more considerate of others and not track mud in here. Now get out of here!"

The two younger children are really confused and whisper together in the yard.

"We saw Dad and Tara taking Mom's cookies," says Susie. "They are being really bad — wait until Mom finds out! She always catches us when *we* do stuff wrong. She even knows what happens when she's not around! Boy, they'll be in trouble, won't they?"

"Dad was sure mad at us for making such a mess," says PJ. "That must be worse than what *they* did. We really are bad kids for messing up Mom's floor. We better do what Dad says and stay out of the kitchen with our muddy sneakers."

Gail comes downstairs, glances up at the cookies, and gets started on supper. Pete winks at Tara, squeezes her arm, and whispers, "Hey, what did I tell you?" Tara is totally confused. She can't understand why her mother did not look more closely to see if there were any cookies missing.

"Boy," says Mom. "What a day I've had. I'm really tired. Am I glad I baked all my cookies yesterday. I really appreciate that none of you touched them. I know it must be tempting, but the weekend will be here before you know it," says Gail.

Pete winks at Tara again when Gail isn't looking. Tara is more confused and anxious as she tries to sort out her feelings. She feels her brother and sister staring at her during dinner, but she can't even look at them.

Tara feels guilty and angry, first at herself, but then at them. "So what if I took some stupid cookies," she thinks to herself. "I'm the one who does everything around here. I deserve some treats. Besides, I'm like one of the adults, and that means the rules are different for us."

On Tuesday, the scene repeats, only this time Pete suggests taking two or three cookies each. Tara is depressed and confused but doesn't let it show. She quickly gives in to her dad's pressure, just to get it over with. And it isn't all so bad. Pete sits with her a while at the table. He tells her again that she's special and reminds her with that big smile of his, "Boy, you sure do enjoy those cookies." The younger children do not come near the kitchen.

When Gail comes downstairs, she looks up at the plate of cookies. This time, she thinks she notices something different. She looks more closely, but isn't sure. Maybe she's just imagining things. After all, who would take them? She knows the younger children can't reach, and surely Pete and Tara would never touch them. "It must be my imagination," she thinks.

During supper, however, she feels irritated and thinks to herself, "PJ and Susie are fighting more than usual. And Tara, who is usually so patient with them, doesn't seem to give them the time of day. And just look at the way Pete is winking and smiling at her. Something must be going on here."

"He used to look at me that way. But then look at the way she cozies up to him and sits so close. I mean, she's practically in his lap. She's too old to do that — it just doesn't look right. She's getting just a bit out of line around here."

On Wednesday, the fourth day, the scene repeats, and Pete and Tara take a couple of cookies each. But this time Gail is sure somebody must have gotten into the cookies.

"Okay, what's going on around here?" she snaps in an irritated voice. "Who is taking cookies? It must be you," she says to Tara. "Or is it you?" she snaps at Pete.

Tara is relieved that the truth is coming out, but before she can say anything, Pete jumps to his feet and starts yelling. "What, are you going completely crazy? You walk around here like a madwoman, yelling at everyone and accusing us of taking one of your stupid cookies."

"I think you've forgotten what's important around here," Pete yells. "You act like cookies are more valuable than your family. Well, I'm important and I deserve some respect around here. I'm sick of your attitude. Maybe I should just leave and go somewhere where I'll get some respect." He smashes his fist into the wall, leaving a hole in the wallboard, before storming out of the house.

Gail cries, "Wait, Pete, c'mon, please come back. You're right. I have been overtired and irritable lately. I'm sorry I even had such thoughts."

Now Tara is really upset. She realizes she can never tell the truth, or Mom and Dad will get a divorce. She feels so ashamed for eating Mom's cookies and breaking her trust, but she also feels angry at Dad for making her do it in the first place.

As she looks back at Mom, sitting in her chair crying, Tara feels even more angry at her. "Gosh, Mom is so stupid. Dad can just say anything and push her around. If Mom had only stuck to her point, the truth would be out. The whole thing could be over, but Mom backs down so easily."

On Thursday, the fifth day, the scene repeats yet again, only this time with some important differences. Tara is irritable when Gail asks if she has her homework done. Tara yells at her, "No, and it's none of your business. What do you care anyway? I hate you."

Gail is upset and yells back at Tara, "Don't you be disrespectful. I'm tired of your moodiness and backtalk around here."

Pete jumps to his feet and yells at Gail, "Oh, get off her back. Stop being such a nag. She does a lot of stuff around here that you don't appreciate."

Angry and depressed, Gail goes to the bedroom to change.

Tara doesn't know what to do. She knows she was wrong to talk that way to her mother, but her dad didn't seem to think it was any big deal, and he stood up for her. She turns and says, "Let's get some cookies, Dad."

Pete pulls back and replies, "No, I don't think we should. Your mom will be really upset if any more are gone."

Tara persists. "Oh, come on, Dad, I think we deserve some cookies. You were right, I really do love them."

"Well, okay, if *you* really want them. I guess a couple more won't hurt," replies Pete. They chew the cookies quickly. Tara turns her head away, hoping her father won't see the tears in her eyes or hear the churning in her stomach.

Meanwhile, Susie and PJ continue to behave badly. They are out of control, fighting with each other in the yard. They don't go near Tara, who picks on them constantly for being such slobs and brats. The younger children continue to feel uneasy and confused, as Pete keeps them outside for longer and longer periods of time. He yells at them whenever they knock on the door too soon.

Susie and PJ do not talk out loud, but thoughts whirl around in their heads: "I hate Tara. Why is Dad always sticking up for her? He loves her more than us. He's always winking and smiling at her, but he just yells at us for being bad. And what about the cookies they took? Dad and Tara must have taken them — we saw them that time. It's not fair! But that couldn't be. I mean, Dad wouldn't do something like that. He's the parent, and he knows what's okay and not okay. We must have dreamed it when we saw them. It must be Tara. Maybe she even tricked Dad into it. She's such a brat lately. I hate her."

Susie and PJ are more and more unhappy. They daydream in school instead of paying attention, and they turn in messy papers. They act out angry feelings at their mother as well as at their friends. The children can't believe that Mom doesn't have a clue as to what's going on — if anything *is* going on: "It's just like Dad says, she's really out of it." And yet, the children have no reason to even mention their feelings. Dad would be really mad at them, and at Mom, too. What if their parents got a divorce? "Besides, it's probably not even what we think it is, so let's just forget about it."

On Friday, Tara is sitting in class, not paying attention, while thoughts whirl around in her mind. When the teacher calls on her, she can't answer the question. Embarrassed, Tara snaps out some answer, acting like she really couldn't care less.

At the class break, she listens to her best friend, Melynda, talk about basketball practice. "Why have you been missing practice all week? The team needs you." When Tara doesn't answer, Melynda talks about her father teaching her to play checkers. "When I was little, he used to let me win at Candyland sometimes, but now he won't let me cheat at all. It makes me mad, but he says I'm old enough to know right from wrong." Melynda asks, "How about you? What do you and your dad do together?"

Tara is feeling sad. She is too ashamed to tell her friend about the cookies. She just stares and turns away to go off to her next class.

"What's with her?" Melynda thinks. "She acts like she's mad at me. What did I do wrong?"

During the next break, Melynda finds Tara without her usual bunch of friends. She is alone at her locker, quietly crying. After a lot of coaxing, Tara tells Melynda about stealing her mother's cookies.

"It's just that Dad keeps pushing and pushing me. I hate that kind of pressure," Tara says. "And it's all so stupid and creepy."

Melynda says, "Tara, the only way you're ever going to feel better is if you tell your mother."

"Oh, Melynda, I know," Tara replies, "but there's no way I can tell her now. Dad stood up for me and yelled at her, and she was so wimpy about it. She only cares about not getting yelled at, and Dad not leaving, not about me telling the truth." Still depressed, Tara again goes off to class.

Melynda is worried about Tara and finally tells the guidance counselor, Mrs. Wheatley, who calls Tara in to talk about it. Mrs. Wheatley tells Tara that she was right to let someone know the pressures she was feeling. The counselor tells Tara that she will contact Tara's mother later that afternoon.

Tara is relieved and frightened at the same time. She doesn't want to go home, but she has to babysit for the younger children.

Just as Gail and Pete arrive home that evening, the phone rings. Gail answers, "Oh, hello, Mrs. Wheatley," then listens as the guidance counselor tells Gail that Pete is pressuring Tara to steal cookies.

Gail hangs up in shock. She is so embarrassed that Mrs. Wheatley and Tara's friend know about all this. Then Gail gets angry and confronts both Pete and Tara.

At first, Pete is angry and denies the whole thing. Then he says that Tara must have misunderstood him, and he would talk to her and set her straight.

Tara, however, admits to her mother that it *is* true. She explains how her dad pressured her to take cookies.

Gail turns her anger on both of them. "Why did you have to go along with it? Why couldn't you have told me first instead of broadcasting it all over school? I'm so ashamed of having a husband who sets me up to look ridiculous and turns my daughter against me."

Gail tells Pete, "You get out of the house. It's not just the cookies. You betrayed my trust. You turned everyone against me. The other kids must have known but didn't dare say anything. You completely forgot about me and our relationship. Instead, you just focused on Tara and on yourself. I'll never be able to trust you again." Pete leaves, and Gail bursts into tears.

Now the whole family is in an uproar. Gail doubts that she should ever take Pete back, but then she worries that she will never make it on her own. Pete will need a place to stay, so the money he usually gives to her to run the household will go to pay for an apartment for himself. How will she ever be able to raise three children on even less money than they have now?

Tara is glad her mother took a stand, but she wishes her dad did not have to move out. She misses him already. She wanted to stop feeling so bad about the cookies, but she didn't want to cause so much sadness and anger. Maybe she shouldn't have said anything. Susie and PJ are glaring at her. She knows they are blaming her for ruining everything. They wish their dad was still home. He had promised to take them bowling tonight, but now that's all been spoiled.

Gail, too, feels lonely and sad this evening. She starts to go to bed but pauses to say, "You know, Tara, I believe your dad pressured you, but you're old enough to know better than to cause this kind of trouble in the family. I have watched you all week, getting cozy with Dad and being so cute. You better get your act together and stop thinking just about yourself."

The next day, Pete stops by the house to talk and to get a few of his things. He moves close to Gail, puts his arm around her, and says gently, "I didn't mean to hurt you, you know I love you. You're the most important person in my life. I guess I've just missed having time with you. You've been so tired lately, and I guess I've felt pushed away. I felt really hurt and angry that you wouldn't give me any of your cookies. You just shut me off completely." His voice sounds so sincere.

"I guess I just wanted to give Tara some of the attention and affection she needs," Pete explains, sounding very earnest and reasonable. "And the whole thing only lasted a few minutes. I knew it was wrong, but sometimes Tara is hard to resist. I mean, it's not like *I* was the one who always thought of it. Just yesterday *she* begged *me* to take a cookie with her. You know how I've always loved your cookies, and Tara is just at that age where she knows how to tempt me to take them when I want them."

Gail stops crying and feels cared about for the first time in a week. She, too, had felt shut out and rejected. She hadn't realized how important she is to her husband —she had actually thought he loved Tara more than he did her. And it is true that she had been tired and irritable and hadn't given him any cookies. You can hardly

116

blame a man for wanting cookies. When men want them, they just have to have them. It wasn't right to deprive him. She leans into his arms. He hasn't been affectionate with her for so long. Maybe they just need to spend more time together. Maybe she needs to be a better wife and take better care of her husband's needs. And it is true, Tara needs some straightening out.

Then she turns to her daughter and says, "Tara, your dad and I have been through enough, and you've only been telling half the truth. Dad should have some counseling if he wants to be part of this family, but *you* are the one who really needs to change if we're going to get along in this house."

Tara is confused, as angry thoughts whirl in her mind: "It wasn't at all like Dad is saying. How can he lie like that? He practically forced me to take the cookies in the beginning. Now he's putting all the blame on me and Mom. If he wanted cookies so bad, why didn't he just go to the bakery?"

As she runs from the room crying, she screams at Pete, "I hate you! I never want to see you again!"

With his arm around Gail, Pete says, "It was just a bad week, honey. Things have been tough at work. Now that I see how wrong it was and how unhappy I've made you, I'll never do it again. You can be sure of it. I know our marriage relationship depends on your being able to count on me as a responsible parent and partner. I understand that it may take a while before you are able to trust me, but believe me, I am changing my ways forever.

"Oh, I can understand how Tara is feeling right now," he says. "She is angry and being a bit oversensitive, if you ask me. It's okay if she doesn't want anything to do with me right now, but I think it's wrong to keep me from seeing the other kids. I'm sure they miss me. How about bringing them to McDonald's later today to meet me for lunch. Hey, I guess I have a right to see my own kids, and they have a right to see me, wouldn't you say? And it's not like I did anything wrong with those two kids." Pete smiles as he gives Gail a hug and leaves.

Gail doesn't know what to do. She does not want to leave Tara alone, but she knows the other kids are anxious to be with their father. She turns to Tara and asks, "Do you mind staying here a while by yourself? The other kids need to spend time with their dad."

PJ and Susie look eagerly up at her. Susie says, "We didn't do anything wrong with Dad, and I don't know why you had to tell anyway. Poor Dad has to be outside the house now, and it's all because of you and your big mouth." Tara slowly tells Mom, "It's no big deal. Go ahead. I don't care anyway."

Gail is uncertain and anxious, but she goes off with PJ and Susie to meet Pete. As they leave, they don't notice Tara looking sadly out the window. They have no idea about all the thoughts going through her mind: "Maybe Mom is right. It is my fault. I never did say no."

Pete is thrilled to see them and gives them all a big hug. "Hey, Susie. You look pretty today. How's my special girl?" He takes her hand and brings her to the chair next to him. Gail and PJ trail behind. Susie smiles to herself as she reaches with her other hand down into her jacket pocket and feels the cookie she's brought for her dad.

Discussion Questions for "Stealing the Family Cookies"

Let's think for a while about this story. Putting aside the idea that this is just about cookies, what do you think about the relationships and what happened inside this family and between the people in this family?

1. Would you describe Pete's, the dad's, relationship with each family member as honest or manipulative? Is he always truthful, or does he use thinking errors?
2. What does Pete say that might be considered "grooming"?
3. How did Pete manipulate Tara?
4. How did Pete manipulate PJ and Susie?
5. How did Pete manipulate his wife, Gail, the kids' mom?
6. What do you think Gail was thinking as she went through the week?
7. What might Gail have done differently?
8. Why do you think Tara didn't tell?
9. Why do you think the younger kids didn't tell?

10. How was Tara hurt by this situation?
    a. How did Pete corner Tara into using thinking errors to adjust to her unhappy situation?
    b. Do you think the hurt will simply stop because pressure to take the cookies has stopped?
    c. How did Pete hurt Tara's sense of self-worth?
    d. In the future, will Tara associate eating cookies with pleasure? Or will pleasure be mixed with stress, a churning stomach, and feelings of fear, distrust, and isolation?
    e. Do you think Tara might avoid eating cookies in order to avoid these painful feelings? Or might she start to eat cookies constantly, trying to get back the pleasure she once got from eating cookies and the special feeling of being loved that she had with her dad?

11. How were the younger kids hurt by this situation?
    a. How did they feel about themselves?
    b. What happened to their relationship with their father? Did he influence their way of thinking so that they learned to use thinking errors about what they saw? About who was responsible?
    c. How did their relationships with Tara and with their mother change over time?
    d. What did Susie learn about how to win her father's attention and affection?
    e. What did PJ learn about his value to his father?

12. How was Gail hurt by this situation?
    a. What happened to her feelings of self-worth and self-respect?
    b. How did the children's respect for her change over time?
    c. How did her relationship with all her children change?
    d. What happened to her relationship with Pete while the cookies were being taken?
    e. Why do you think Gail chose to believe Pete's version of what happened? Did Pete's manipulation work so that she too began using thinking errors?

13. What do you think Pete should do to make restitution for the harm he has caused?
    a. How can he begin to repair the harm he has done to self-worth?
    b. How can he begin to repair the harm he has done to relationships?
    c. How can he help change the existence of thinking errors in the family?
    d. How can he help rebuild his children's ability to trust their instincts to know when something is wrong?
14. What similarities, if any, do you notice between this situation and the one you are in now?

You might want to go back and underline all the thinking errors, or photocopy the story and give it to other members of your family to see how many thinking errors they can find. Learning to recognize thinking errors means being able to recognize manipulation. And being able to recognize manipulation means being better able to protect yourself and your family and keep safe.

14

"Borrowing the Family Car": A Story of Youthful Manipulation

The following story illustrates a typical interaction when an older child has the ability to manipulate and persuade a younger child. In many families where sexual abuse occurs, the abusing person is an older child or adolescent who has manipulated and persuaded a younger sister or brother, cousin, close friend, or neighbor to cooperate with the sexual activity. The abusing person may have a caretaking responsibility with the younger child, perhaps as babysitter or camp counselor. If this is the situation in your family, you may be wondering if the sexual abuse that has been identified is just "normal childhood curiosity and experimentation."

It is natural to have confused feelings when children have been involved in sexual activities. Children are naturally sexually curious and often create situations in which they explore their sexuality. If you look carefully at the relationship and the differences between the children, you will have a better sense of whether the situation is just experimental or is seriously abusive — where one child has influence and control over another. Some differences between the children are obvious, such as age or size, but other differences are not so obvious. Answers to the general questions below (as well as to the more specific questions in Appendix A) can provide guidelines for evaluating the relationship.

- Do people consider them "equals," or does one child have more influence or power?
- Do they have equal ability to chose whether they participate in the sexual activity?
- Does one child clearly have more resources, such as money or toys, and therefore more ability to persuade or bribe or force the other child into activities?
- Which child is more likely to listen to the other in most situations?

It is the use of power to get sexual contact that determines when a relationship is abusive. Power can come from many sources, including age, knowledge, maturity, authority, popularity, or access to money. If a careful assessment indicates that an abusive relationship exists, it is important to identify how the abusing child manipulates the other child and the other family members.

When one older or more knowledgeable child sexually abuses another child, there is a strong tendency to look at the situation as less serious than when it occurs between an adult and a child. There is a tendency to think,

"They're just kids" or "They were just fooling around" or "They were just experimenting" or "They were both at fault."

If you are parent to both the abusing child and the victimized child, you might have a particularly hard time facing the fact that abuse occurred. You may want to keep the family together. You may *want* to think of the sexual abuse as "something that just happened" and won't happen again. Thinking this way, however, would not be helpful to you or your children and could interfere with treatment. Thinking this way avoids the hard work of looking closely at the abusive relationship for elements of control; thinking "it just happened" assumes that the less powerful child and the abusing child are equally responsible.

Sexually abusive behavior is not the kind of behavior that just goes away. It's not something that a child will "grow out of," like sucking a thumb or carrying a security blanket around. Many adult abusers began when they were teenagers or even younger.[1] Their behavior did not just go away. It is a mistake to think of sexual abuse as just an incident or a stage-of-life happening or a response to one stressful event.

Sexual abuse, even with youthful and adolescent abusers, involves manipulated relationships and an invisible, secret web of control. It is not an accident—it is done on purpose. It usually grows out of a preoccupation with sex. Without treatment, even if the sexually abusive activity stops for a while, the patterns of manipulation and dishonesty continue and become the way the abusing child approaches relationships and life in general now —and later as an adult. Like adult abusers, young and adolescent abusers can cause serious harm to younger children and to their family relationships. Like adults, younger abusers must be held responsible for repairing any psychological and emotional harm and for learning self-control over their own behavior so they do not spend a lifetime manipulating and abusing others.

In the previous story, we looked at the psychological and emotional damage that occurs in a family when one adult has the power to manipulate and control relationships for his or her own purposes. Let's now look at how similar harm can be done in families when youngsters or adolescents are able to manipulate others.

Read this story with an eye toward discovering hidden signs of injury, manipulative patterns, and the roles that each family member plays in a situation where an older child is able to abuse a position of power and authority and violate the adults' trust.

(Note: If the abuser in your family is not an adolescent, you might want to skip the next story for now and go to Part Four.)

Borrowing the Family Car

It is a typical week in the life of the Johnsons. Both parents, Paul and Beth, work long hours at jobs that barely pay enough to support a family of four. They try to be home for their children as much as possible, but there are a few hours each day when the children are left alone. Paul and Beth have taught their son Gary, who is 15, to be a responsible and reliable babysitter for his brother Ben, who is 8. Gary has been babysitting after school since he was 12.

At first Gary didn't mind because babysitting meant he had someone to play with after school, and it was part of how he earned his allowance. For the past few months, however, he has stopped playing with Ben and just watches television. It's boring to stay home. He would rather be out with his friends, going to the mall or just hanging around downtown. He resents having this child-care responsibility, but he really doesn't have a choice.

His parents understand how Gary feels, but they also feel there's no other choice. Money is tight. It would cost too much to pay for someone else to babysit for Ben, and he's just not old enough to be on his own after school. Paul and Beth need to own two cars, because their work schedules are often different. Whenever possible, however, they ride to work together to save money on gas. This particular Monday morning, Paul and Beth have the same work schedule, and the children are getting ready for to school.

"Well, kids, your mother and I will be home today by 5:30. Try to get all your homework done after school. Perhaps tonight we can go to the mall to get those sneakers you need, Gary," says Paul.

"And please remember to put the chicken I've fixed in the oven at 4:30 so that it will be ready when we get home," says Beth. "You know, Gary, it means a lot to us that we can count on you to take care of things here at home while we're at work. We trust you to be in charge and to be responsible so that Ben gets his homework done and doesn't get into any trouble. And Benny, we really appreciate your listening to and obeying your brother and not giving him a hard time." With that, the parents drive off together to work and the children go off to school.

After school, Gary and Ben have snacks and watch a little TV. Then Ben goes to the kitchen table to start his homework. Gary is restless and paces around his room looking for something to do. A few minutes later, Gary comes over to talk to him.

"Hey, Ben, this sitting around all the time is getting pretty boring, don't you think?" says Gary.

"What do Mom and Dad think — we've got nothing better to do? Most kids can have *fun* after school, but no-o-o, not us. Hey, I have a great idea! But it would have to be a big *secret*. Oh, well, no, never mind. I guess you're not old enough yet."

"Oh, come on, Gary, you can tell me," Ben pleads. "I *am* old enough for secrets. I'm not a *baby*. Come on, please, let's do your idea." Ben is definitely interested. He thinks Gary is a great brother. He misses the time Gary used to spend with him.

"Oh, I don't know. I mean, this is a *big* secret. You couldn't tell Mom or Dad. It's not anything bad, but you know how Mom and Dad are — they think we should just sit around here. But we could do something and still have plenty of time to get our jobs done," says Gary. "Do you really think I could trust you to keep this big, exciting secret?"

Ben nods and tells him, "I can keep a secret, Gary, really I can. See?" And he runs his finger across his mouth like a zipper and then puts the make-believe key in his pocket.

"Okay, then. This is it. We can take the car for a little drive down the street. Mom and Dad won't know anything, and it would be such fun, wouldn't it? Dad used to take me out to practice, but he's been so tired lately. He never has time. Besides, how am I ever going to be ready for my license test if I don't spend time practicing?"

Ben is shocked. He doesn't know what to say. He didn't expect the secret to be anything like this. Ben looks at Gary's face, all excited and smiling. But he knows it would be wrong and that their mother and father would be really angry. He knows their parents trust them. "But Gary, I don't think we should do that. We would get in such big trouble. Besides, I have a lot of homework. I'm having trouble with math and the teacher says I should spend extra time."

Gary says, "I should have known you were too little. Crumb, I'm not talking about going away for hours. I'm talking about taking a short drive around the block and back. No big deal. Just to practice my driving. Believe me, Mom and Dad will never notice. They never notice half the stuff around here. I mean, my sneakers have had holes for months. But they don't even notice."

Gary keeps talking. "I'll put the car back exactly where they left it. And we'll only be gone a few minutes, so you can still get your homework done. You know, I'm getting sick of this family. All they expect from me is work, work, work. It's not fair! Dad has promised for a week to take me driving, but he forgets. I can't count on him. I thought you were different, that you and I could be pals and have some fun like kids are supposed to." He starts to go to the other room to watch TV.

Ben is confused. Gary is right in some ways. Mom and Dad are always tired, and it's true, they don't notice lots of things. They don't always keep their promises right away, but then again, they really do try to keep their promises whenever they have the time and money. Gary looks so disappointed and angry. It isn't fair that he never has fun with his friends, but I can be fun, too, Ben thinks. He hasn't asked me to do anything with him for a long time. I guess it wouldn't hurt to go just this once. "Okay, Gary. I'll go with you."

Gary is excited. They run outside and get into the car. Slowly, Gary backs it out of the driveway. As they drive down the street, he has a big smile on his face.

"You're all right, kid! In fact, you're terrific. Some of my friends have such jerks for brothers. But you're a real pal. And besides, this sure is fun, isn't it?"

Ben has to admit it is kind of exciting riding down the street with no parents in the car. And it is fun being with Gary. "I just hope none of the neighbors see us," he thinks to himself.

Gary drives around the block and goes back home. He does just what he said he would do. He had put a stick on the driveway marking the spot so he could park the car in exactly the same place. They go inside and do their homework.

When their parents get home that night, they never notice a thing. After supper, Paul turns to Gary and says, "Okay, let's go. You can drive to the mall. I'm sorry I've had to work so much lately and haven't had time to take you out to practice for your driving test. I know how important that license is to you. Maybe we can go out another night this week and get you those new jeans you need, Ben."

Gary smiles and gets up, but Ben's stomach churns and he's got a big lump in his throat. He just looks down at his lap.

A few days later, Paul and Beth again have the same schedule and drive to work together. That afternoon, Gary and Ben sit down with their snacks to watch some television.

After a few minutes, Gary stands up. "Let's go. Let's get out of this boring place. Let's get us some action. Today we could take the car to the park. It's not that far. And we could get ice cream cones. I saved some of my lunch money for a treat. Let's go!"

Ben is confused and anxious all over again. Gary looks so excited and happy, and he wants to treat for some ice cream. But the park is eight blocks away.

"Gary, I don't think we should go," says Ben. "I mean, Mom and Dad trust us. I just wouldn't feel right. I really have to study for a big spelling quiz. And Dad did take you driving the other night. It would take too long to go to the park, and they'll notice if the car is moved."

"Are you kidding?" Gary can't believe he's arguing with him. "I told you, Mom and Dad don't notice things like that. I mean, did they notice anything Monday? No-o-o. They just think about work all the time. Besides, it won't take much gas at all. Sure, Dad took me driving once, but it will be weeks before he gets around to it again. And I really need to practice, so I can get my license and get a part-time job. I know Mom and Dad work hard, but I'm old enough to start helping out. And besides, aren't you tired of the same snack, every single day? I think we deserve a treat, don't you?" Gary puts his arm around Ben's shoulders. "Come on, just the two of us. We had such fun the other day. You loved it as much as I did."

Ben is nervous and can feel a knot in his stomach. But he doesn't want to make Gary sad or mad. Gary is probably right. Mom and Dad won't notice anything, and he really *is* trying to be helpful and thoughtful.

"Oka-a-ay," he slowly agrees. "Let's go." And off they go.

Gary is in such a hurry, he forgets to mark the exact spot in the driveway where the car was parked. When they arrive at the park, they get out and go to the ice cream stand. Gary orders them each a cone. They wander over to the swings and sit while they eat.

Ben eats his cone quickly, but Gary is not in a hurry. "What's the rush? We've got a couple hours before they get home. Let's climb on this gym set. I can show you some tricks."

Ben reminds Gary of his spelling quiz and asks if they can go straight home. Gary turns and looks angry. "So, what is it now? Are you going to be a little baby and have to go home?" he sneers. "You know, there's more to growing up than going to school and doing homework all day. Have you ever even heard of having fun?" Gary rants. "What a stick-in-the-mud you are. Just because Mom and Dad don't know what it means to have fun, doesn't mean we kids can't have any. But if you want to be a jerk like the other guys' baby brothers, go ahead. Oh, just forget it. Let's go home, just like the little baby wants."

He gets up and stalks off toward the car, leaving Ben to trudge along way behind him. Ben is really upset now. He doesn't know what to do. He wants to go home, but he doesn't want to spoil things with his brother.

"Wait," he yells to Gary. "You're right. It won't hurt if we stay a little longer."

Gary turns and smiles. "Are you sure?" he asks.

"I'm sure," says Ben.

They stay for over an hour. Gary drives home fast and not very carefully. Ben is scared but doesn't dare say anything. They get home just a few minutes before their parents arrive. Ben tells Gary he isn't parking in the right spot. He tells Ben not to worry, their parents won't notice.

When Beth and Paul arrive home, Ben is at the kitchen table with his homework. Gary is just starting to put the supper in the oven to heat. Before Beth can speak, Gary says, "Sorry, Mom, I was so wrapped up in my homework that I didn't even realize the time and forgot to put supper in the oven."

Beth is surprised, but not angry. "That's okay, Gary. We can just eat a little later today. I'm glad you were getting your studying done. You are so responsible. I'm so proud of you."

Their father goes to his chair to read the newspaper before supper. Ben is really puzzled now. He always thought their parents could tell when one of them was lying, but Gary is getting away with it. They didn't even notice the car was in a different place. Boy, Mom and Dad *really are* out of it. Gary is right. They don't notice what's really going on.

The next day, Paul and Beth again have the same schedule and go to work together. As soon as the children get home from school, Gary says to Ben, "Okay, we're out of here. Let's go to the beach today. Come on, we can bring our kites and get another ice cream cone."

Ben is nervous and timidly says, "Gary, that's really too far to go to the beach. It will take a lot of gas, and you know Mom and Dad are trying to save on gas."

Gary smiles and says, "Ben, you worry too much. It won't take that much gas. Mom and Dad won't even notice." Ben slowly walks out the door and gets into the car.

When they get to the beach, Gary helps Ben with his kite. They run up and down the beach for a long time, then eat their ice cream cones before going home. On the way home, Gary says, "Wasn't that the best fun ever? Boy, you really had a great time. I could tell you liked it because you were laughing a lot." As he pulls into the driveway, Gary again is not careful about where he parks. Again, he does not have supper ready.

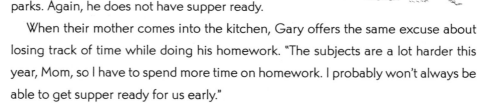

When their mother comes into the kitchen, Gary offers the same excuse about losing track of time while doing his homework. "The subjects are a lot harder this year, Mom, so I have to spend more time on homework. I probably won't always be able to get supper ready for us early."

Beth pauses for a few minutes. She feels uncomfortable, as if Gary were telling a lie. "Oh, but that's ridiculous," she thinks to herself. "Why would he lie?" She turns slowly and says, "Well, I understand, Gary. I'm just glad to see you taking your studies so seriously."

A little later his father comes into the kitchen. "You know, I could swear I parked that car on the other side of the driveway. You weren't fooling around with the car, were you, Gary?"

Gary turns to his father and says angrily, "Why would I touch the stupid old car? Where am I going to go with it? I don't have my license, and it's no big thrill going up and down the driveway. Boy, that's the thanks I get. I come home every day to babysit, and you accuse me of touching the car! I just hate living in this house."

Beth says, "Wait, Paul. Think about it. Gary has been so dependable. Do you really think he would betray our trust? He's been busy with homework all afternoon. I can't believe what you're saying. Besides, who else do you think we could trust looking after Ben?" Paul glares at Beth but then shrugs his shoulders, apologizes to Gary, and offers to take him driving later.

Ben is amazed and angry. Their parents *don't* know what's going on! They are just plain stupid. Why does Dad back down like that? If he thinks Gary has used the car, why doesn't he go look at the gas gauge? Or check the car's floor mats? There's sand all over the place from the beach. His brother is right. Their parents really *are* out of it.

When Beth goes to see how Ben's homework is coming along, she notices that he has barely started. "Ben, what have you been doing all afternoon? The teacher called me today at work and said your grades are dropping and that you're not getting your homework done. I'm very disappointed. I trust you to get your homework done in the afternoon. I won't be able to take you to get jeans tonight because you need to spend the time on the homework you didn't do this afternoon."

Ben jumps up from the table, slams his notebook closed, and starts yelling. "Homework is a stupid waste of time. What do you care, anyway? I hate you." He runs to his bedroom and slams the door.

"I wonder what's gotten into him," Beth says to Gary. "I wish he could be more like you and just do his work without having to be told." She gives Gary a hug.

On Saturday, Paul has to work in the morning, so Beth decides to drop him off while she does some shopping. "If you can just babysit for a while this morning, Gary, you can be free to spend the afternoon with your friends. Ben, I don't want you to give Gary a hard time like you've been giving me. I just don't know what's gotten into you lately. It's not fair to be acting this way when Gary gives up his time to take care of you." Gary stares at his brother. Ben feels a knot in his throat but doesn't say a word.

As soon as their parents are gone, Ben turns and says, "Hey, Gary, let's go for a ride. I feel like another one of those great ice cream cones."

Gary goes to turn on the television, saying, "Oh, I don't know. We don't want to push our luck too far. I mean, we're in this together, but Mom and Dad might get more suspicious."

Feeling angry and upset, Ben goes to his room. Soon Gary comes in and says, "Okay, I guess you're right. We do deserve a treat today. Mom's really been on your case lately, so I can see why you'd want to go out. Let's get going. Who knows how long we have before Mom gets home."

Ben again is confused about what he wants to do. He doesn't want to get in more trouble, but he's feeling so lonely and angry. It's not fair that Gary doesn't stick up for him. Boy, he sure knows what to say to get *himself* out of trouble.

"Hey, c'mon Ben, don't sulk. Let's go for a ride, favorite brother of mine." Gary grabs Ben's hand, and they run to the car. They spend a couple of hours at the beach, flying kites and climbing around the rocky shore. They again get home just before Beth and Paul pull into the driveway. Beth goes directly inside, but Paul tells her he needs to get a hat that he left in the other car.

Suddenly, Paul storms into the house. "Okay, now I want the truth. The car is parked in a different spot in the driveway, and half a tank of gas is gone. There's sand all over the floor. What's going on, Gary?"

At first, Gary is speechless. Ben is scared, but at the same time, he is relieved that the truth is finally coming out. Then Gary says, "Okay, I did take the car out. I know I shouldn't have, but Ben really wanted to go. You know how he's been, and I felt sorry for him. He seems so unhappy lately. I'm sorry I broke your trust this one time. I promise I'll never do it again. You can count on me. When I make a promise, I stick to it."

Mom and Dad are shocked that Gary has betrayed their trust — and broke the law by driving without a license — but they also know how awful Ben's behavior has been lately. Even the teacher has been complaining. "Well, Gary," says Beth. "We are extremely disappointed in your lack of good judgment. Doing something illegal and dangerous by driving without a license and without enough experience just to please someone else is not setting a good example for your brother."

"You are the older one and should know better," says Paul. "I know it's been hard for you lately, but I've got to be able to count on you in the future. It'll take a while before we can trust you again."

Then Beth turns to Ben and says, "You had better start acting more responsibly around here. It's not fair to put that kind of pressure on Gary."

Ben is very upset. He can't believe that Gary put all the blame on him. He can't believe that their parents believe Gary and aren't even asking him what happened. They act like they love Gary more than they love him. Ben bursts into tears and screams, "I hate you all!" He runs to his bedroom.

"And don't slam . . ." Beth starts to say, when the crash of the door sounds.

Paul sighs and turns to unpack the groceries. "Well, Gary, I understand why you did it, but I'm still angry that you broke our trust. You could've gotten a ticket if you'd been stopped. Not to mention that you put yourself and Ben — and our car — in danger. Well, since nothing worse happened, you're grounded for a week."

Beth adds, "Since you're going to be here, I want you to help me out. I ran into Aunt Mary at the supermarket. She's coming over this afternoon with your cousins, Tim and Emily. I'd like to count on you to help entertain the younger kids."

Gary didn't have any plans with his friends anyway, so he responds, "Oh, sure. I'd be glad to help out."

Later, while his mother and aunt are busy talking in the kitchen, Gary plays baseball out in the yard with his cousins. Ben just stays in his room all day. Paul has gone over to a neighbor's.

After a while, Beth asks Gary to babysit for just an hour or so while she and Aunt Mary run to a sale at the mall. "No problem, Mom. Take your time," says Gary.

After they have been gone a while, Gary turns to his cousins and says, "Hey, do you kids want to take a ride to the park?"

———————

Discussion Questions for "Borrowing the Family Car"

Now let's think about this story. Putting aside the idea that this is just about an irresponsible teenager, what do you think about the relationships and what happened inside and between the people in this family?

1. Would you describe Gary's relationship with each family member as honest or manipulative? Does he speak the truth, or does he use thinking errors?
2. How does Gary get Ben to cooperate?
3. Why do you think Ben feels responsible — and guilty?
4. What percentage of responsibility would you assign to Gary? To Ben? To the parents?
5. Why didn't Ben tell? How did his use of Gary's thinking errors ease his bad feelings?
6. Why didn't Gary own up to what he'd been doing the first time he was questioned?
7. How was Ben harmed in this situation? What happened to his relationship with his parents?
8. How were Paul and Beth, the parents, harmed in this situation?
9. What do you think the parents ought to do differently?
10. What do you think Gary should do to make restitution for the harm he has caused?
11. What similarities, if any, do you notice between this situation and the one you are in now?

You might want to go back and underline all the thinking errors, or photocopy the story and give it to other members of your family to see how many thinking errors they can find. Learning to recognize thinking errors means being able to recognize manipulation. And being able to recognize manipulation means being better able to protect your family and keep children safe.

Note

1. Abel, G. G., & Rouleau, J. L. (1990). The nature and extent of sexual assault. In W. L. Marshall, D. R. Laws, & H. E. Barbaree (Eds.), *Handbook of sexual assault: Issues, theories, and treatment of the offender* (pp. 9–21). New York: Plenum.

Hindman, J. (1988). New insight into adult and juvenile sexual offenders. *Community Safety Quarterly, 1,* 3.

part four

Treatment and Restitution

I5

Thinking About Treatment: Repairing the Hidden Hurt

Perhaps after reading the stories "Stealing the Family Cookies" and "Borrowing the Family Car" you have a better understanding about how hidden emotional and psychological injuries can occur when one person in a family is able to control and manipulate others. In these stories, one person's secrets and manipulations injured every family member's emotions, thoughts, and beliefs. When one person in the family manipulates others and sexually abuses a child, hidden emotional and psychological injuries occur in the same way. Recognizing that real harm has been done is the first step in the victim's and the family's healing from the abuse.

The next step is to use this information to determine what can be done about abuse in the family — to learn which things can change and which things cannot. Think for a minute about how you might react in other situations when something valuable is not working quite right. Would you just throw it out? You might, if you didn't care. Would you try to fix it yourself? Surely, some things that you know about, you can repair yourself. But when it's a bit more complicated, you may take the item to a specialty store where experts can fix it for you. Or you might take a class where you can learn how to make repairs like an expert.

Sexual abuse is not the kind of problem that you can fix by yourself. It is not even the kind of problem that experts can just "fix." With sexual abuse, experts need your help to understand your family. Then the experts can work with you to figure out how to repair the hidden injuries and, if you are the abuser, to stop acting in controlling and abusive ways.

Trusting in Treatment: What Good Does Talking Do?

It is not unusual to question whether talking about thoughts and feelings can possibly do any good. You may be thinking that the sexual abuse is over and that talking about it won't change anything. Some people you know may even think that treatment (also called counseling or therapy) is bad for you and for your family because the talking just seems to make everyone feel worse.

It's true that facing and talking about painful matters can make people unhappy for a while. But in families where abuse has occurred, people were already unhappy — it's just that no one was talking about it. Would your situation be any different right now if bad feelings around the abuse could have been talked about? What if the first moment the abuser had thoughts about sexually touching a younger person, he or she could have told someone. Imagine how your family might be right now if everyone could have understood the seriousness of the abuser's behavior and had insisted that the abuser receive treatment right away. Or, what if the first time the child was abused, he or she had told someone who could hear about the abuse calmly and knew who to call and how to help the child by stopping the abuse sooner?

Avoiding talking about facts, thoughts, and feelings may be causing pressure inside the people you love and contributing to your family's unhappiness right now. The next metaphor compares feelings that people store inside themselves to bubbles stored inside a soda bottle. Try using this situation to explain to children how talking in their counseling sessions can be an important step toward changing family behavior patterns.

A soda bottle can sit on a shelf for months with thousands of bubbles stored unnoticed inside. But if that bottle is shaken up before it is opened, the soda spills all over the place when you try to pour it. You can't get the cover back on until almost all the bubbles are released.

It's the same with you and your feelings. They may sit inside where no one can see them, but if something happens to shake you up, the feelings may come out in uncontrollable ways—perhaps as anger in different directions, at different people, and not even toward the person you're really angry at.

But imagine opening that same bottle gradually. It wouldn't matter how many bubbles were inside, you could open the soda carefully, release the pressure, and cap the bottle again whenever you wanted to.

That's like you and your feelings, too. If you could talk about your thoughts and feelings a little bit at a time, you could have more control over how you feel and release the pressure inside you a little bit at a time.

The need to talk about upsetting events is nothing new. People do it all the time with one another when they share an event or when they believe they will get support for their feelings. When you've had a bad day at work or school, doesn't it usually help if you get to talk about your feelings?

Think about how people react after a loved one has died, or after traumatic events such as tornadoes or fires or life-threatening accidents. They tell the story over and over, talking about the details of the event, often to many different people, until almost everyone knows what happened. This is a normal, healthy way to decrease upsetting feelings caused by a traumatic event. It's a way of getting over the pain of it, while holding the event safely in memory.

Sometimes talking with friends and family is not enough. There may be powerful feelings that require professional help to deal with. Sexual abuse is this kind of problem. That's really where counseling begins: learning to figure out your thoughts and feelings not just about sexual abuse but also about other problems, as well as the good things in your life. You might use talking, drawing, writing, or some kinds of playing as ways to think about things and reduce pressure by letting out your feelings.

Once you feel less pressure, it may become easier to figure out how you can handle some of the problems in your life. You may be able to make some changes that will help you feel better and allow life to go along more smoothly. A counselor can help you make these changes.

16

....

Selecting Treatment:
The Need for Specialized Counseling

Coping with the enormous upheaval caused by sexual abuse in your family is one of the most difficult tasks you will ever face. Because the problem of sexual abuse is so complicated, it can be difficult to treat. For that reason, it is important that you and your family get help from trained professionals who can provide *specialized* sexual abuse treatment for children who've been abused, for siblings, for nonabusing parents, and for abusers. In this part we review important aspects of treatment, some of which have already been mentioned earlier.

Attending counseling sessions by itself will not make your home safe for children. Treatment works only for people who put in the extra time and emotional energy required to make lasting change. It works only for family members who believe that there is a serious problem and who truly want help. It works when you are willing not only to *notice* when something seems "off" — or even when someone handles a hard situation well — but also to *talk* about it out loud to the rest of the family and the therapist. Good treatment is about clients and therapists working together to uncover all the facts, to assess the degree of harm, to find ways to repair the hidden injuries to each family member, and to notice and support it when people have done the right things or done a hard thing well.

Counseling can help your family increase its understanding of the abuse and resolve powerful emotional reactions. Counseling can help members of your family emotionally and mentally detach from the invisible control web spun by the abuser. Remember our earlier discussion of the parallel between the spider's web and the abuser's web: just as the spider depends on its web to catch bugs, so the abuser depends on a carefully planned web of secrecy and manipulation to abuse young children. The way for families to prevent most sexual abuse is to learn to recognize parts of the abuser's *control web*; to release themselves from attachment to this secret, invisible web; to rebuild a healthy, open, connecting family web; and to avoid any other control webs in the future.

Counselors can help members of your family find out whether there are any "blinders" that need to be removed, talk through their feelings, and return their "radar" to full operation. Counselors can help any unhappy children in your family find ways to feel better about themselves and learn ways to protect themselves in the future. And counselors can help nonabusing parents become better protectors of their children through better understanding of themselves, the abused child, the siblings, and the abuser.

Counselors can help sexual abusers work through their denial and their resistance to facing the facts. Abusers have quite a job ahead of them. Just to learn to manage their own behavior they must accomplish at least the following seven steps[1]:

1. Confront their denial and fully admit their abusing behavior.
2. Recognize and decrease their use of thinking errors and manipulative patterns.
3. Identify their risk factors.
4. Increase empathy for their victims by understanding and taking responsibility for the harm they have caused.
5. Increase their social skills and learn new or strengthen existing nonabusive activities and interests.
6. Work to decrease their deviant arousal, understand their cycle of abusive behavior, and develop a relapse prevention plan.
7. If and when appropriate, explore the impact of the abuser's own childhood victimization.

In addition, sexual abusers who want to repair the harm they have caused — *whether or not they will be reunifying with their victim and their families* — need to do one other extremely important thing[2]:

8. Explain to their victim and family members how they engaged and abused a child, what harm they caused, and how they controlled other family members. This clarification will help family members, both children and adults, not to be fooled or manipulated again.

While in specialized treatment, highly motivated abusers can work to get rid of their old secret, invisible webs, the ones where they got their emotional needs met by using and manipulating others. With a lot of hard work, abusers can learn to build a healthy, visible, connecting web of life, one where they get their emotional needs met by connecting with and caring for others and developing self-control. Developing this open, visible web is really the only way that relapse prevention plans will work.

Later on in Chapter 19, "Treatment for Abusers," we'll spend more time looking at how relapse prevention plans work. But first, we're going to look at the very important work that happens in treatment with a child who has been abused.

Notes

1. Murphy, W. D., & Smith, T. A. (1996). Sex offenders against children. In J. Briere, L. Berliner, J. A. Bulkley, C. Jenny, & T. Reid (Eds.), *The APSAC handbook on child maltreatment* (pp. 175–191). Thousand Oaks, Calif.: Sage.
2. Hindman, J. (1989). *Just before dawn*. Ontario, Ore.: AlexAndria Associates.

17

Treatment for Abused Children: Victims and Siblings

Now that the abuse has been disclosed and has ended, you may wish at times that the victim could put the abuse in the past and "get over it" so life could settle down. Many children cannot "just get over it" and go on. Remember that all along, during the abuse, it was not easy or even possible for the child to separate from the abuse or the abuser. Even though the abuse is no longer secret and is no longer happening, the child may not be able to separate from the feelings and memories connected to the abuse.

Some children do not experience upsetting memories of their abuse or are able to put them into perspective and go on with their lives, but many abused children become preoccupied with memories of the abusive events. Other children look just fine on the surface, but underneath they have hidden emotional struggles. And still other children show by their moods and behavior that they are deeply affected by the abuse and by all the reactions to its disclosure. It is difficult to tell just by looking at children how they have been affected by the abuse. Sexually abused children have learned over a long period of abuse how to cover up and look different on the outside from how they are feeling on the inside. Remember, what isn't opened up and healed now is likely to surface in the future.

We have to look inside the emotions of children who have been abused to understand how they are coping. Abused young children and adolescents may turn their feelings inside themselves, tend to feel depressed or anxious, withdraw from other people, or have suicidal thoughts or commit acts of self-harm. Others may act out: fighting with friends or family, being mean or bullying toward siblings or classmates, breaking school and family rules. Some may reenact their own abuse by sexually acting out toward younger children or oversexualizing their behavior with friends and older persons. Some children may try to numb their pain by using alcohol or drugs or by letting their bodies be used sexually over and over by others. Privately and secretly, many of these children still feel the troublesome feelings and think the distorted thoughts that they had and learned during the abuse.

Specialized treatment helps the child move through this experience from being a victim to becoming a *survivor* of abuse who has learned to cope in constructive ways.[1] Victims who grow to adulthood without counseling frequently continue to suffer emotional pain from their abuse. A major treatment goal for the abused child is to greatly increase the child's ability to cope successfully with the emotional pain that memories and thoughts of abuse bring up.

The full *trauma assessment* (discussed earlier) gets information about the details of the abuse and looks at whether the child has had a traumatic reaction to being abused. That information helps the therapist decide what kinds of treatment will help the most.

One of the first steps in counseling is to help abused children get a clear picture of their abuse and work out some of the powerful emotions that arise from it. Before disclosure, the abused child in your family may not have been able to find a way to talk about what was happening, so all the feelings about the abuse probably stayed locked inside the child's mind or came out in nightmares or in behavior.

Sexual abuse doesn't fit into normal family behavior. The stories a child reads in school, the experiences of the child's friends, the TV shows and movies the child watches don't include abusive sexual activities. When there is no place in a child's mind to put memories as part of normal experience, the thoughts and feelings about the abuse can keep playing over and over. It's as if there's no file drawer in the child's mind to put the thoughts into. Abused children often feel powerless to get rid of these potentially traumatic thoughts, emotions, and memories. The child may still be connected or "bonded" either to an identity as a victim or to the relationship with the abuser. These memory connections are referred to as the victim's *trauma bond* with the abuse. Sometimes these memories and emotions are so powerful and so painful for the abused child that they become life-threatening. A child may feel that suicide is the only way out of the pain, or the child may use other self-destructive behaviors, such as drug or alcohol abuse, to numb the pain.

To understand how sexual abuse can trigger strong emotional reactions, think about another strong force that can both attract and frighten at the same time: fire.

Fire warms us and draws us to it by its light and dancing flames. But it can burn, so we have to keep a lookout to make sure it doesn't get out of control and hurt us. So it is with a child who must keep a constant lookout for his or her abuser, always trying to protect himself or herself from the next sexually abusive action. It is this need for constant guardedness and watchfulness that trains the child to pay attention to thoughts and feelings connected to the abuse, even after the abuse is over. It is like the experience of watching an endless-loop 3-D movie with Surround Sound: the special effects are so strong that even after the movie ends, the scenes keep playing over in the viewer's mind.

Because these highly charged emotional memories may have existed within the child for a long time, they do not easily get filed safely away. Resolution may require many counseling sessions over months or even years. Children can be released, at least in part, from these feelings by learning how the abuser manipulated them during the abuse. Instead of feeling still tangled up in the sticky, abusive web, a child can cut the cords and wash off the stickiness. Through therapy and family support, abused children can replace feelings of shame and guilt with feelings of pride and self-respect, knowing that they are not responsible for their own abuse.

One of the most important goals of therapy for abused children is to separate the negative feelings associated with sexual abuse from the positive feelings associated with normal, healthy sexuality. When the traumatic feelings related to the sexual abuse are resolved, the "3-D movie" becomes just an album of faded photographic memories to be put on a shelf and taken out only when needed.

145

There are many ways children can get drawn into a continuing trauma bond with their abuse. Children have sense memories of their abuse in their skin, in the parts of the brain that process the things they see and hear and smell and taste. There are also feeling memories and thought memories.[2] Children may think of themselves as "damaged goods," or others may relate to them that way.[3]

Children may remember and worry about their own (or the abuser's) sexual responses during the abuse. Children who had sexual responses may develop guilt and shame associated with sexual fantasies that include elements of the abuse. Children sometimes believe (or were taught) that they were responsible for attracting the abuser and causing the abuse. Children may feel overly responsible, believing that they should have stopped it or disclosed it. Or, they may feel that they should not have disclosed it and caused the family or the abuser so much pain.

Children may be unable to ask any questions of or express any negative emotions toward a parent or other nonabusing caretaker who did not protect them or keep the abuse from happening. Like the younger siblings PJ and Susie in the story about stealing the family cookies, most children see their caretakers as powerful and all-knowing — even about the secret abuse. If their caretakers don't stop it, that must mean that the parent thinks it is all right. Children's wishful thinking that the nonabusing parent could have stopped the abuse is often present, even in situations where it wasn't realistic. Most children in abuse situations aren't able to call out in actual situations of danger. They are forced to push these wishful feelings, along with many other feelings, down inside themselves or to act them out through anxious or disruptive behavior.

All or some of these thoughts may create a confusion of feelings and a trauma bond with the sexual abuse. Dissolving the power of that bond is an important part of treatment. How children recover from abuse depends on many things that are different for each child, including the degree of force, violation, invasion, stimulation, emotional and mental manipulation, or type of control the abuser used. For some sexually abused children, it is difficult to manage their feeling-memories when the abuser controlled them through threats or other fears. For other children, it is difficult when the abuser controlled them through gentle and tender ways, taking advantage of pleasurable physical or sexual responses in the child.

To be released from their shame and guilt, abused children must understand the ways they were controlled and manipulated. Recovery also requires support from the people most important to abused children: their family. Whether children can keep from developing a trauma bond, or be released from it once it develops, depends on whether they can get help to resolve all their emotional, mental, and physical attachments to the abuse.

This next metaphor may demonstrate the importance of releasing the child, not from memories of the abuse but from the powerful emotions connected to those memories. Picture what happens when a person tries to get out of another kind of dangerous or abusive situation. Imagine yourself in an airplane that has been flying along with engine trouble for quite some time. You are worried and want the pilot to land the plane, but the pilot assures you that everything is under control and insists that you just be quiet. Finally, you are sure you are in danger and decide to get out of the plane. You hunt around until you find, in a hard-to-see place, a parachute. You put it on, gather up all your courage, take a deep breath, and jump out. Even though you have gotten out of the dangerous airplane, you are now in another dangerous situation related to, or connected to, the troubled airplane. You may not know much about parachutes or how to land safely. You may want to pull one way to avoid going into buildings and trees and another way to go toward a big, open field. You will stay in that uncertain situation until you are safely on the ground. If you come down in a really good environment, you will land where there is a ground crew prepared to assist your release from the parachute and away from its power to hurt you when strong winds are dragging you along the ground. The crew can help you check over your parachute to find any weak spots that need repairing and then help you fold it up and put it away in its storage sack. It's your parachute, so you can keep it to look at any time you want to think about the experience. But you don't have to wear it on your back, dragging you down as you go on with your life.

Now picture such a parachute for a child who tries to bail out of a sexually abusive situation, only to find himself or herself in yet another uncertain, potentially hurtful situation. There are many points where the child, even while escaping from the abuse, remains attached, through memories, to the sexual abuse and thus to the relationship with the abuser. Often children become confused after the "bailout," or disclosure. At times, children pull in the direction of their *angry* feelings toward the abuser and the nonprotecting parent, but at other times, they pull in the direction of their *pleasing* feelings, wanting to regain the affection of the abuser or of the nonabusing parent. Sometimes children wish they had not bailed out at all. After the bailout— the disclosure—the new situation often looks even worse, scarier and more dangerous, than the sexually abusive situation itself. This can happen when sexually abused children have no ground crew to help release them from the power of their memories to hurt them. When disclosing children find themselves alone, without strong family support and without knowledgeable help, they may get hurt more. They may continue to suffer even though the abuse has stopped.

That is why it is so important to be doing what you are doing in treatment: learning as much as you can about sexual abuse, about your children, and about yourselves, so you can help the abused children in your life keep from being bound by the traumatic feelings around their sexual abuse. The family, the community, the protective workers, the treatment providers, and the prosecutors are the "ground crew" that can help children land safely after disclosure. To be safe and free from trauma bonds, the abused child has to *dissolve the power* of all those feelings, thoughts, and memories to cause emotional pain. This does not mean forgetting about the abuse. Like the parachute that gets inspected before it is carefully folded and stored, the memories of the abuse can be talked about and "inspected" for areas that still hold power and thus need resolution before they can be carefully stored away. The abused person will still have the memories, but they will be faded memories without power to hurt the abused person anymore. Through this process of thinking and talking about the abuse, the child reduces the power of the memories to cause emotional pain. The child leaves behind the intense emotional pain of having been a victim and gains the good, proud feelings of becoming a survivor of abuse.

Strengthening a Sense of Self-Worth

Specialized treatment provides a way to understand how the abuse hurt the child and what is needed for the child to feel better and safer. One of the most important reasons to help a child reduce the painful effects of abuse memories is to make room inside the child's mind and heart for good feelings and thoughts about himself or herself. In therapy sessions, some by themselves and some with their families, children who have been abused can understand what happened to cause such hurt. They can find ways to feel stronger and be proud of who they are. And they can learn ways to try to protect themselves from abuse in the future.

We've looked at a lot of the ways children who are abused may become confused and unsure of their own worth.[4] Through all the manipulations, abusers usually give children many different messages about whether they are valued. When abusers give a lot of attention, affection, and special favors in return for sexual activity, for example, children may believe that they are loved only when they are sexual.

Other family members, often out of their own confusion or anger or sadness, may also give the abused child the message that he or she is not loved or is the main problem in the family. Think back on the stories you read earlier and try to recall all the negative feelings that were expressed to Tara and Ben. In "Stealing the Family Cookies," Tara's brother and sister were not getting any loving attention while the stealing was occurring. They naturally became jealous and resentful and blamed Tara, not their father. Tara's mother, Gail, became uncertain of herself and resentful toward Tara for getting the father's attention all the time. In "Borrowing the Family Car," Ben's mother didn't see Gary's manipulations and expressed a lot of disappointment in Ben. She even blamed Ben for pressuring his older brother to break their trust. It's as if the brains of each of the "nonabusing parents" and the siblings were fighting to keep out any new information about the "abusing person" being irresponsible. It was too hard to make this new information fit with the picture in their minds of how they wanted and needed to see the "abusing person." So at first they blamed the "victim" in their families.

In both stories, Tara and Ben were responding to their natural need for love and attention. It seemed that the only way they could get it was by giving in to demands to do something they didn't want to do and understood was wrong. At some previous time, their "radar"—their sense of right and wrong—had been working well. But under the pressured persuasion of the "abusing persons," Tara's and Ben's radar became confused and jumbled and eventually stopped working.

Instead of being encouraged in activities that increased pride in their achievements and self-confidence in their self-worth, Tara and Ben were encouraged to participate in activities that brought them a sense of shame and feelings of guilt for the wrongdoing. Remember Tara's uncertainty: "Maybe Mom is right. It is my fault. I never did say no." Even after the cookie stealing and car borrowing were discovered, both Pete, the dad, and Gary, the brother, continued to avoid responsibility and manipulated their families to blame Tara and Ben. It's no wonder that abused children sometimes feel very lonely and sad inside during the abuse, and even worse after it all gets disclosed. Sometimes anger from others makes them feel unloved and just plain bad inside.

Sometimes family members are too hurt and confused themselves after the disclosure to be able to give the support that abused children need. In these situations, it's particularly important for children to be in a counseling situation where there is a focus on repairing and strengthening family relationships and on helping abused children remember all the wonderful things about themselves.

Treatment for Siblings: Regaining a Position of Importance

We've looked at how brothers and sisters or cousins of the abuser are often confused by what has gone on during the abuse. After disclosure, when there is so much focus on the child who was abused and on the abuser, the individual needs of the brothers and sisters or cousins may be overlooked by family members and even by treatment providers.

Think back to some of our stories and remember some of the effects on those who were not directly involved in the hurtful activity. In the story of the Captain who ignored the ship's radar signals, the crew members became anxious and afraid and gradually lost the use of their own personal "radar" that informs them that something is wrong.

In "Stealing the Family Cookies," PJ and Susie questioned their own self-worth, as they were yelled at for sloppiness and pushed outside to play. Their "radar" sent jumbled signals. At first, they understood clearly that what their father was doing with Tara was wrong. But that way of thinking about their father was confusing and frightening. They looked to their mother to straighten it all out but were further puzzled that she didn't seem to know about it and didn't do anything to fix it. With no one to talk to, the two children developed behavior problems as they acted out their fears. They talked back to their mother and fought with other children. In an attempt to regain a positive image of their father, they took on his distorted way of thinking, his thinking errors: first, that *they* were thoughtless children, dirtying up the house; then, that *Tara* was to blame for getting their father in trouble and causing the family's unhappiness.

What happens in these stories is similar to what happens in families where sexual abuse occurs. Order in the family is lost when people in authority break the family rules and begin a pattern of mistreating others. Treatment helps siblings as well as children who have been sexually abused regain a sense of their self-worth, the use of their instincts to know right from wrong, and the ability to manage their emotions and their behavior.

To protect themselves in the future, siblings need to understand all the ways the abuser manipulated the abused child, the nonabusing parents, and themselves. Because the siblings lived in a family where there may have been many confusing messages about sex and intimacy, siblings as well as the abused child may need help learning about healthy sexual relationships. Sibling needs should be an important part of family therapy, as everyone works to put order back in the family.[5]

Notes

1. Hindman, J. (1991). *The mourning breaks: 101 "proactive" treatment strategies for breaking the trauma bonds of sexual abuse.* Ontario, Ore.: AlexAndria Associates.

2. Hindman, J. (1989). *Just before dawn.* Ontario, Ore.: AlexAndria Associates.

3. Sgroi, S. M., Blick, L. C., & Porter, F. S. (1982). A conceptual framework for child sexual abuse. In S. Sgroi, *Handbook of clinical intervention in child sexual abuse* (pp. 9–37). Lexington, Mass.: Lexington Books.

4. Friedrich, W. N. (1995). *Psychotherapy with sexually abused boys: An integrated approach.* Thousand Oaks, Calif.: Sage.

   Friedrich, W. N. (1990). *Psychotherapy of sexually abused children and their families.* New York: Norton.

   Hindman, J. (1989). *Just before dawn.* Ontario, Ore.: AlexAndria Associates.

5. Meinig, M. B., & Bonner, B. L. (1990). Returning the treated sex offender to the family. *Violence Update,* 1, 1–11.

18

....

Treatment for Nonabusing Parents and Families: Regaining a Power Balance

As the partner of an adult abuser, or as the nonabusing parent of an abused child or of an abusing child or adolescent, you hold an important key to the recovery of your family. As we've recognized earlier in this book, one of the the biggest factors in whether abused children get over the effects of sexual abuse and start feeling better about themselves is whether members of their family believe and support them. And often the biggest influence on whether abusing adolescents or abusing adults stick with the hard work of treatment is the presence of a nonabusing parent who holds them responsible for learning to control their problem behavior and repairing harm to the family.

If You Are the Nonabusing Parent of an *Abused* Child

If you are the nonabusing parent of an abused child, you can play an important role in your child's recovery. You can be aware of all the ways the abuse might have affected your child and other family members. You can be aware of the possibility that while the abuse was going on, your child might have engaged in wishful thinking that you could have stopped the abuse. This wishful thinking may have been based on other thoughts—that you knew or should have known about the abuse. You might have engaged in that same kind of thinking: wishing that you could have known about or done something about the abuse while it was occurring, or feeling that you *should* have known and done something.

An important part of all your children's recovery will be your steps in rebuilding their confidence in your ability to protect them. One way to do that is to let them know that you understand their wishful thinking, that you are working in treatment to see whether there were any "blind spots" in your radar and to take responsibility if there were any way you might have better protected them. Many nonabusing parents are not responsible for missing signs of abuse and manipulation, such as when the abuse happened far away or the child did not show obvious signs of abuse. Even then, it is still important that these children know that their parents understand their sadness or anger at their parents for not protecting them. It is important for all children to hear from their nonabusing parents that they are learning better ways to detect when an abusive situation is occurring. When nonabusing parents let their children know all this, they increase the likelihood that their children will develop confidence in their ability to protect them in the future.

If You Are the Nonabusing Parent of an *Abusing* Child

The nonabusing parent of an abusing child has one of the hardest yet most important jobs in determining whether that child gives up manipulative and sexually abusive behaviors. When you are the parent of both the abusing and the abused child, your job is especially difficult, as you may want to be supportive of and helpful to both children. And when you are the parent of just the abusing child — the aggressor — you do not always receive family or community support for the emotional pain you are experiencing.

When other members of your family or community direct anger toward your child for abusing someone younger, you might understandably feel protective of your child. You may even want to minimize or deny what your abusing child has done. But it is important for you to thoroughly understand the nature of your child's abusing behavior, as well as the effect of this behavior on the child who was sexually abused. Then you will be in a much better position to help your abusing child accept responsibility for his or her behavior and work to repair the harm he or she has done to the abused child and to others in the family. That's how parents do their job in other areas of child rearing: they help their children recognize what they have done wrong and what they need to do about it.

A Balance of Power

There is another very important reason for you, as a nonabusing parent, to hold the abusing adult or adolescent responsible for all the effects of the abuse: you need to free yourself from any control the abuser may have over you. One of the reasons ongoing abuse can occur in a family is that in some areas of family life there is an unequal balance of power in favor of the abuser: the nonabusing parent's power decreases as the abusing person's power increases.

This power imbalance is not always easy to see. When the abuser is an adult partner, the abuser may blame the nonabusing parent for creating problems in their relationship. Instead of working on having intimacy and equality in the adult relationship, the adult abuser gets his or her needs for pleasure and power met by manipulating the nonabusing parent and other family members and by taking advantage of a child. The nonabusing parent often loses confidence as a parent and self-esteem as a sexual partner. When the abuser is an adolescent, he or she usually lives under the parents' authority but again gets his or her emotional needs for power, pleasure, or affection met by manipulating the nonabusing parents and other family members and by taking advantage of a child.

Adolescent and adult abusers may control the nonabusing parent through thinking errors, pressure, demands, temper outbursts, persistent pleading, demonstrations of (usually short-lived) sorrow and remorse, and even fear. The abusing person may back the nonabusing parent out of his or her position of authority by using anger or statements that manipulate the parent. Again, think back to our earlier stories. Pete was able to back Gail off and jumble her "radar" by suggesting that something had to be wrong with Gail to make her so suspicious and so possessive of her cookies, and then by threatening to leave her alone with all the child-care responsibilities. Gary was able to back off his parents by reminding them how much he did for them babysitting every day, by pointing out Ben's recent behavior, and by playing one parent off against the other. You can probably understand that when abused children and siblings see adults' inability to stand up to the manipulations of the abusing person, it is hard for these young children to imagine a way to assert themselves against the abuser's manipulations.

Treatment for the nonabusing parent is based on findings of an individual *needs assessment* in the early stages of treatment. If you are the nonabusing parent, it is important to learn how you have been hurt, to enhance all the good parenting skills you already have, and to learn what you need to do to strengthen your position of authority in the family and to reestablish a sense of order and safety in your home.

Thinking about a seesaw might help us envision the difference between balanced and unbalanced power between an abusing person and a nonabusing parent. Imagine a playground bully using his or her bigger size to weigh down one end of a seesaw and thus control a smaller person on the opposite end by keeping the person frightened, unsure, and suspended high in the air, unable to touch the ground.

In a similar way, a family abuser might load down his or her side of the relationship "seesaw" with persuasive thinking errors and manipulative actions. The abuser then controls the nonabusing parent by keeping this parent confused, unsure, and "suspended" in an ineffective place, unable to touch the "ground" of what's really going on in the family.

On a playground, the seesaw can come back in balance in two ways: (1) the bully can give up some weight advantage by choosing to move toward the middle or by dropping a heavy backpack, or (2) the smaller person can gain some weight advantage by moving as far back on the board as possible or by getting help from other people.

The balance of power in the abuser–nonabusing parent relationship can come back in balance in similar ways: (1) the abuser can give up some control advantage by getting rid of thinking errors and other controlling behaviors, or (2) the nonabusing parent can step back from the relationship, join together with others, and see more clearly so that thinking errors have no "weight," that is, no ability to control.

Looking at it this way, with the metaphor of the seesaw, we can see that the
nonabusing parent often has the most
ability to control and improve the situation: even if the abusing person doesn't
want to give up control or the relation-
ship, that side of the seesaw automatically
loses "weight" and power once the nonabusing parent learns to recognize manipulative thinking errors and asks for help.

The nonabusing parent's treatment involves a lot more than learning all about the manipulations of abusers and the effect of sexual abuse on children.[1] The nonabusing parent's treatment focuses on rebuilding self-esteem, developing more assertive ways for overcoming manipulations and standing up to the abuser, and making changes that reassure the children that their nonabusing parent will be better able to protect them in the future. If there is any plan for the abuser to return to the family, the nonabusing parent will have to become an expert in awareness of the abuser's behavior cycle and relapse prevention plan.

Note

1. Deblinger, E., & Heflin, A. (1996). *Treating sexually abused children and their nonoffending parents: A cognitive behavioral approach.* Thousand Oaks, Calif.: Sage.

Meinig, M. B., & Bonner, B. L. (1990). Returning the treated sex offender to the family. *Violence Update, 1,* 1–11.

19

....

Treatment for Abusers

Whether you are an abuser, a nonabusing parent, or a child affected by sexual abuse, it can be helpful to understand how complicated treatment is for sexually abusive behavior. There is no quick fix. If the abuser has been abusing repeatedly, it has probably taken a long time, often years, for the problem behavior to develop and become this intense. There are several stages of treatment for the problem of sexually abusive behavior: (1) admitting responsibility, (2) assessing risky behavior, (3) recognizing injury to others and learning empathy, (4) getting rid of thinking errors and learning corrective behaviors, (5) learning healthy sexual arousal and developing a relapse prevention plan,[1] and (6) *restoring* the family and others through explaining about the abuse and the manipulative patterns used. Restoring the family is often called "restitution." Explaining to family members about abuse and the abuser's own manipulation patterns is often called "clarification."[2]

The abusing person *earns* his or her right to enter treatment, as well as to move on to the next stage, based on the ability to show progress. Although there is not enough space in this book to give details of each of these stages, we do need to think about the progressive and interwoven nature of treatment. No single promise or change ensures that the abuser will stop. Rather, it is a combination of factors, each one strengthening the other, that offers the most promise for effective treatment.

An abuser's treatment plan is based in part on a complete sexual history and a thorough assessment of the abuser's potential for reabuse. This information helps determine whether the abuser can be safely treated in the community. When abusers take on complete responsibility for the abuse, they begin developing the capacity to recognize and try to repair the harm they have done to their victims and families.

Before abusers have the right to be with children they have abused, they must prove to their treatment providers that they are making these key changes in the ways they think and behave and in the way they relate to the world.[3] This means a major change from the way the abusers thought, believed, and behaved before and during the abuse. A major change means that abusers must work hard to meet their own needs, not take the easy way and use children to meet their need and desire for power, control, and sex. Abusers must stop seeing people as property to be used. Abusers must recognize their patterns of disrespecting the boundaries of others. Abusers must learn to see people as separate individuals with their own needs and desires and their own right to say no to any violation of their boundaries. And further, abusers must recognize their responsibility as the older, more knowledgeable person *not* to do anything that might be harmful to a child, whether or not the child says no.

A major change means that abusers must be able to identify every time they use manipulative distortions in their thinking — whether dealing with car mechanics, or resolving conflicts with coworkers, or manipulating children who have the right to an abuse-free life. These habitual thoughts and behaviors are not just about sexual abuse; they are about a life pattern of doing things "my way" and not following the rules. Each time they recognize a thinking error that avoids responsibility and manipulates or blames someone else, abusers must demonstrate a readiness to correct the distortion as soon as possible. The sooner the correction follows the distortion, the closer the abuser is to living an honest, nonmanipulative life.

In order to keep from abusing again, sexual abusers must learn to recognize the repeating pattern of thoughts, decisions, events, and feelings that have become part of their cycle of abuse. When events repeat in a pattern, we can predict with some confidence what will happen in the future. Some things have a more evenly predictable cycle: the hours of the day are evenly spaced, and midnight comes around exactly every 24 hours. Some things

are less predictable: rain and snowstorms occur periodically throughout the year, but they don't always bring the same amount of precipitation every year. People have cycles. Everyone eats, sleeps, and wakes on a more or less regular basis, but everyone has his or her own pattern. Some people have moods that come in cycles and affect their behavior. Sometimes these cycles seem unpredictable, and so do the behaviors. Yet, a close look at these cycles often reveals a predictable pattern.

Sexual abusers who abuse over and over repeat their behaviors in cycles. In order to learn how to control their abusive behavior, abusers must first recognize the *predictable patterns* of their own individual cycles. Second, they must develop action plans to stop themselves from going through their abusive behavior patterns again (called "relapsing"). Such a plan is called a *relapse prevention plan.*[4] Having—and using—a relapse prevention plan doesn't guarantee the abuser won't abuse again, but it gives the abuser a strong mental tool to control his or her behavior around children. When the abuser's detailed abuse cycle and relapse prevention plan are shared with family members, they can be aware of predictable behavior patterns to watch for so they can protect their children.

Specialized treatment can help abusers develop such behavior-control plans. Although there are individual differences, some basic ingredients are common to all cycles and relapse prevention plans. Let's look at some *predictable* parts of a typical *abusive behavior cycle.*[5]

Feelings about what is going on in life do not cause someone to sexually abuse children. It is the way the abuser *thinks* about *what to do* about the problem or feeling that causes the person to abuse. The abuser makes a decision to feel better by using others in a sexual way. Sexual abusers do not take the positive step of handling their feelings constructively or solving their problems. No one can always control feelings, but most people can learn to control their own actions.

For sexual abusers who don't receive treatment, the reinforcing feelings and thinking errors connected to the sexual behavior are stronger than any preventive feelings and thoughts. The abuser acts out his or her pattern of abusing others more and more often, until it becomes a habit that is hard to control without a lot of specially trained help. The abuser becomes stuck in a cycle of abuse.

Fortunately, no one has to stay stuck in a cycle. There are many places during the cycle that the abuser can choose to think or act differently. First, sexual abusers have to admit that they have a serious problem. They must recognize the *thinking errors* involved in their cycles. They also must recognize their patterns of making little decisions that don't seem like they're part of the problem but in fact lead up to the problem behavior. These are called *seemingly unimportant decisions* (SUDs) and are part of the predictable behavior cycle.[6] If abusers recognize all the little decisions that lead up to the big decision to sexually abuse, they can identify many points where they could decide *not* to do something that is part of the cycle. In this way, they can interrupt their cycles and control their abusive behavior.

Life is full of problems to be solved and corrected. When people use problems as *excuses* to give up their efforts to make things better, then their problems take control. Everyone feels powerless once in a while when they are unable to solve a problem. But sexual abusers think of problems as excuses to feel better by using children sexually. These problems then become part of their abuse cycles.

Many behaviors have cycles that include predictable patterns. To under-

---

Cycle of Abusive Behavior

- a **problem** going on in life (such as failing in school, losing a job, having trouble making friends or getting along at home)
- **feelings** related to the problem:
  - emotions inside that make the person feel bad or angry or worried
  - feelings of powerlessness, hopelessness; feeling sorry for oneself
- **feelings** related to sexual arousal: want to make self feel better, in control
- **fantasies** about sexual behavior:
  - may include lots of masturbation, use of pornography
  - begins to include fantasies about someone to *control* for sex: a child
- use of **thinking errors** to make sexual abuse seem okay and to *control* others
  - stuck in feelings of powerlessness about problem situation
  - blame others such as the teacher, the boss, the other kids, the abused child
  - ever-increasing need for power and control
- actual **planning** of the abuse; includes grooming the victim
- acting out the fantasy; committing **sexually abusive behavior**
- possible **deterrents** (preventions) to abusing again:
  - feelings of shame about self; guilt; feeling bad for the abused child
  - self-promises not to do it again
- **reinforcers/rewards** to abuse:
  - *pleasure* from sexual arousal and behavior; often includes orgasm
  - feelings of *power* from control of others
- **cycle begins again:**
  - feelings of guilt, low self-worth from abusing child, powerlessness, hopelessness

---

stand more clearly how the repeated habit-forming behaviors of sexual abusers are hard to change, let's look at a behavior pattern that most people recognize. Notice the *thoughts,* the *feelings* and the *seemingly unimportant decisions* (SUDs) that Bill makes during his cycle of an out-of-control problem behavior.

Bill's Story

Bill's doctor has told him that he must lose weight. Bill recognizes that part of his weight problem is that he eats when he *feels* overtired and depressed. He also knows that his biggest weakness is his passion for ice cream, especially chocolate almond ice cream. He can resist other fattening foods like cookies and chips, but he's always had a hard time sticking to a diet because he has not been able to resist overeating ice cream [problem behavior]. So he goes to the freezer and throws out all the ice cream [one way to stop (deter) the problem behavior]. Bill also knows that there are two things he must do to keep himself focused on his health and losing weight: get regular exercise and avoid getting overtired [other deterrents to problem behavior].

For the first week or two, Bill stays on his diet. He feels good about himself because he feels in control. He exercises every evening after work and gets a good night's sleep. Then one morning his boss tells him that he's not satisfied with one piece of work and gives it back to him to do over [problem]. Bill feels *upset* [feelings]. He *decides* not to look at the work and puts it in a pile to do later [SUD]. He feels irritated all day. He starts thinking how his boss doesn't recognize what a good worker he is. After all, he even stays late sometimes to finish projects. "No matter how hard I try," Bill thinks, "I can never please him. He always treats the other workers better than me" [series of thoughts].

By the end of the day, Bill has decided not to redo the work [SUD] and thinks to himself that he'll do it tomorrow [thoughts]. He leaves feeling tired and irritated [feelings]. On the way home, he plans to buy something to cook for supper, but he decides to drive by his usual supermarket and go to the one that carries his favorite ice cream [SUD]. He thinks to himself that he's not going to buy any; he just likes this store better [thoughts].

As he pushes his cart down the aisles, instead of going past the frozen food aisle, he decides to turn down toward the ice cream section [SUD]. He decides to go to the low-fat frozen yogurt section [SUD], thinking to himself that he needs a treat today, after all he's been through [thought]. But when he looks at the yogurts, nothing appeals. He decides to push his cart past the ice cream section, looking at all the flavors [SUD]. At first, nothing appeals. Instead of moving on, he decides to let his eyes rest on the chocolate almond flavor [SUD]. He decides to reach for the container [SUD], thinking to himself, "Hey, I've been strong all week. I'm fine. But there's no reason not to bring some good ice cream home for the kids" [thoughts].

Later that evening, Bill thinks about his boss and how unappreciated he feels [feelings]. Somehow he doesn't feel in the mood for exercising tonight [feelings] and decides not to go for his usual evening walk [SUD]. He decides to go to the refrigerator for some juice, but then looks at the freezer door. "Hey, why not?" he thinks to himself. "I didn't have any bread with dinner, so just a taste won't hurt." He decides to get a spoon, push it into the ice cream, and put it into his mouth [SUD].

All the old sensations of pleasure associated with chocolate almond ice cream come rushing back [feelings]. He decides to get a bowl out of the cupboard [SUD] and dishes himself up a large serving of ice cream [beginning problem behavior]. "Ah, that tasted great, and it felt good to have a treat," he says to himself.

But a little while later he feels bad about breaking his commitment to stay away from ice cream [feelings]. "I'm so weak. I'll never lose weight," he starts to think. "Hey, wait a minute, it's not my fault. Everyone needs something good in his day. My boss is way too critical" [thoughts]. But Bill feels lousy about himself right now and wants to get rid of that feeling. He decides to return to the refrigerator [SUD] and dish up another serving [the out-of-control problem behavior]. "Ah, this is just what I need. I feel better just thinking about it" [feelings] he tells himself as he decides not to think anymore about his problem at work and decides to settle down with his ice cream to watch a late-night talk show. When his wife comes to say good night, she notices his huge dish of ice cream. He looks up, shrugs, and says irritably, "Hey, don't get on my case, it was just an impulse. I've had a tough day and I need to relax before I go to bed. Don't worry, I'll get back on my diet tomorrow."

Bill's story shows how someone can avoid taking responsibility for a problem and blame others. It shows how not correcting or solving a problem can lead to thoughts and feelings that cause other problems, thoughts, and feelings. It demonstrates how seemingly unimportant decisions and reinforcing pleasurable feelings can lead to a *relapse* into unwanted behavior.

As you look back at the story, you can find many points where Bill could have changed his attitude and made different decisions that would have kept him on track with his plan not to relapse into overeating. Even after his first bad decision of not correcting the problem at work, for example, he could have recognized his pattern of feeling sorry for himself and stopped at the first store instead of going to the one that carried his favorite ice cream. Even if he hadn't recognized that he was in his cycle of unwanted behavior until he got home, he still could have decided not to eat the ice cream or even to throw it out. When he thought about his boss, he could have recognized his self-pity and made the decision to redo the work first thing in the morning.

This story is about an out-of-control cycle of behavior that mostly hurts Bill but could hurt others too, such as his boss, who needs the job done correctly, and his family, who depends on him to keep his job and to stay as healthy as possible. If Bill wants to stick to his commitment not to overeat, he could develop a relapse prevention plan that might look like this:

Bill's Relapse Prevention Plan

- Problem behavior: overeating
- Assessment:
  - Harm from overeating: overweight, risk of high blood pressure, type 2 diabetes
  - Identify points in the cycle of the problem behavior:
    - Temptations leading up to behavior: all ice cream, but especially chocolate almond ice cream
    - Reward of overeating: pleasure of taste and feeling full
    - Precipitants to behavior: sensitivity to criticism, mood swings, feelings of worthlessness or rejection, anger
    - Recognition of thinking errors (thoughts twisted around the truth) to justify problem behavior: avoiding solving the problem, blaming someone else, self-pity, rationalizing, minimizing responsibility, telling his wife and himself that it was an impulse.
- Deterrents to behavior:
  - Remove temptation from the home (remove ice cream)
  - Develop exercise plan
  - Get a good night's sleep
  - Be aware of seemingly unimportant decisions that lead up to overeating
  - Decide to face and solve problems.

The sexual abuser's story is about an out-of-control behavior cycle that mostly hurts others, but also hurts the abuser. It's not easy to give up this behavior, which has strong, reinforcing sexual feelings. But it is possible. It's up to abusers to work hard in treatment to understand their problem and recognize the seemingly unimportant decisions that lead up to abusing children. These decisions might include deciding to drink or use drugs or to look at pornography. They might include deciding not to face a problem at work or at school. They might include deciding to feel sorry for themselves instead of analyzing their problems and solving them. Such decisions probably include getting themselves into situations, or even setting up situations, in which they can be alone with children. Each abuser's story is different. Treatment providers will not be able to help abusers stop abusing unless the abusers first decide to be honest about their cycles of behavior. This is how a cycle of sexual abuse might look on a chart.

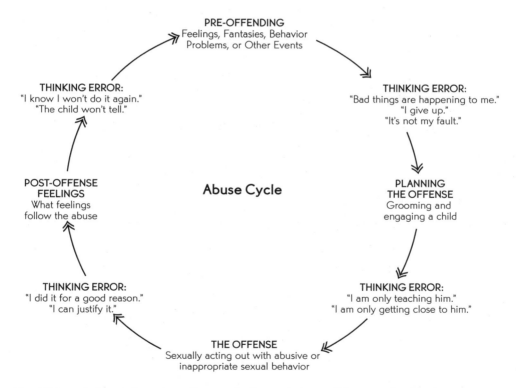

PRE-OFFENDING
Feelings, Fantasies, Behavior
Problems, or Other Events

THINKING ERROR:
"Bad things are happening to me."
"I give up."
"It's not my fault."

**PLANNING
THE OFFENSE**
Grooming and
engaging a child

THINKING ERROR:
"I am only teaching him."
"I am only getting close to him."

THE OFFENSE
Sexually acting out with abusive or
inappropriate sexual behavior

THINKING ERROR:
"I did it for a good reason."
"I can justify it."

**POST-OFFENSE
FEELINGS**
What feelings
follow the abuse

THINKING ERROR:
"I know I won't do it again."
"The child won't tell."

Abuse Cycle

Note: This cycle is an adaptation of many similar variations of abuse cycles, but is particularly informed by Tim Kahn, *Pathways: A Guided Workbook for Youth in Treatment* (Brandon, Vt.: Safer Society Press, 1996).

Are Abusers Really Treatable?

Major change is a difficult task for anyone. Major change for someone who uses and sexually abuses children is extremely difficult, but not impossible. There are many effective treatment programs offering methods for changing behavior. But major change in sexual abusers is possible only for those who recognize the harm they have done to the spiritual cores of others, as well as to themselves. Major change is possible only when abusers are able to create a change within their own spiritual cores. As mentioned earlier in the section on recognizing the hidden harm, a person's spiritual core may or may not include religion, but clearly it includes those feelings, thoughts, and values that give depth and richness to the human condition. A spiritual core raises the human being above other life-forms, such as plants or animals, and allows people the capacity to care for and connect with others.

Real change is possible only for abusers who can give up their old ways and adopt new ways to meet their emotional and psychological needs for pleasure, power, control, companionship, intimacy, and a sense of being loved. Real change is possible for abusers only when they are committed to letting go of a distorted, unhealthy lifestyle organized around getting their needs met through the sexual abuse of children and the abuse of others. Further, abusers must adopt a purposeful, healthy lifestyle reorganized around the commitment to never again meet their needs through the abuse of another person — child or adult. These changes can be especially difficult for abusers who think of themselves as being kind and loving, as "soul mates" with their victims.[7] By letting go of the need for power and control over others, abusers can develop a life pattern of self-control and respect for all people, including themselves.

If you are the partner, parent, or child of an abuser — or if you are an abuser — it is important to understand how difficult change can be for anyone, but particularly for people who sexually abuse children. People who abuse others are treatable only when they understand and accept the need for hard work and a deep commitment to change through treatment.

Sometimes abusers find it easy to stop abusing while they are in the supportive atmosphere of treatment. The real test of whether treatment has been effective is whether the abuser can keep from going back to abusive ways, or relapsing, after treatment ends. Looking once again at the metaphor of a spider's web might help you picture how many parts of the abuser's life must change in order for treatment to work.

Remember that webs exist naturally for drawing connections and supports between people and between parts of our lives. But a person who sexually abuses children weaves a very different kind of web. Instead of a visible, open, connecting web, the abuser's web is invisible, secret, and controlling.

First let's take a closer look in the next illustration at the abuser's secret web—an abuse-*producing* web. Each part of the web is connected to and reinforces the other parts. A "lack of respect" for self and others, for example, feeds into "denying the abuse," which in turn feeds into "doing poorly in treatment." And a strong need for "control of others" and an "unhealthy lifestyle" are linked to difficulties in family relationships and to a "negative inner spiritual core." You might use this web-diagram as a checklist to think about how the abusing person in *your* situation conducts his or her life. This web might also be helpful in assessing both the strengths and the areas of difficulties in the abuser's relationships with you and with other family members.

This abuse-*producing* web helps us to see that although the abusing person may have some strengths and positive parts, there are many more negative parts that need to change to create a healthy, open, visible, connecting web—the abuse-*preventing* web. A successfully treated abuser who works hard in treatment could learn to weave this new kind of web, one that is focused on getting emotional needs met through a commitment to never abuse another child. The next diagram of an abuse-*preventing* web shows such a web carefully planned and woven by the abuser to prevent himself or herself from returning to abusive ways. This web-diagram is a way of picturing the holistic changes in all areas of life that are needed to help the abusing person develop and support a strong *relapse prevention plan*. The abuser won't be able to permanently give up his or her behavior if he or she changes only one part. Just giving up an unhealthy lifestyle of substance abuse, for example, or just going through all the steps of treatment is not enough. Each part of the abuse-*producing* web needs to change so that each part of the newly developed abuse-*preventing* web connects to and strengthens

Abuse-Producing Web

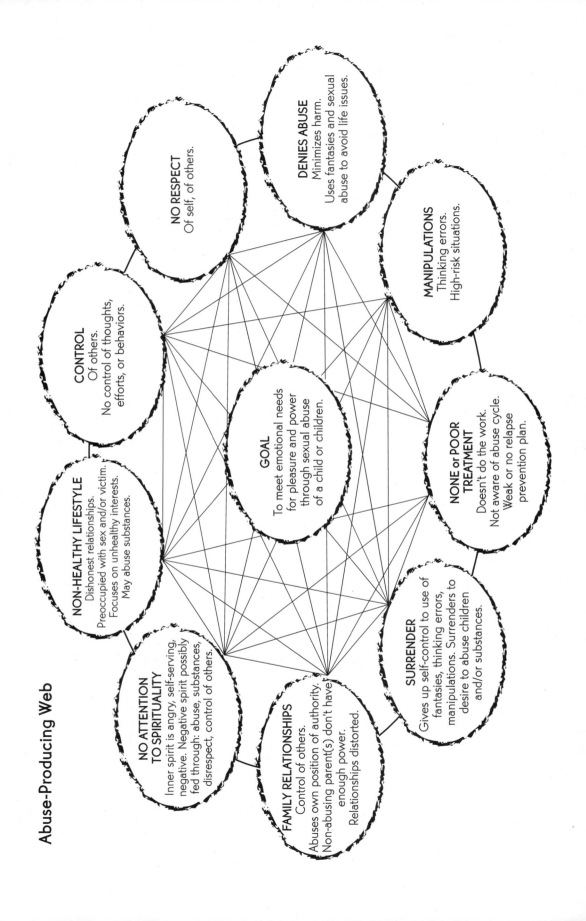

DENIES ABUSE
Minimizes harm.
Uses fantasies and sexual abuse to avoid life issues.

NO RESPECT
Of self, of others.

MANIPULATIONS
Thinking errors.
High-risk situations.

CONTROL
Of others.
No control of thoughts, efforts, or behaviors.

GOAL
To meet emotional needs for pleasure and power through sexual abuse of a child or children.

NONE or POOR TREATMENT
Doesn't do the work.
Not aware of abuse cycle.
Weak or no relapse prevention plan.

NON-HEALTHY LIFESTYLE
Dishonest relationships.
Preoccupied with sex and/or victim.
Focuses on unhealthy interests.
May abuse substances.

NO ATTENTION TO SPIRITUALITY
Inner spirit is angry, self-serving, negative. Negative spirit possibly fed through: abuse, substances, disrespect, control of others.

FAMILY RELATIONSHIPS
Control of others.
Abuses own position of authority.
Non-abusing parent(s) don't have enough power.
Relationships distorted.

SURRENDER
Gives up self-control to use of fantasies, thinking errors, manipulations. Surrenders to desire to abuse children and/or substances.

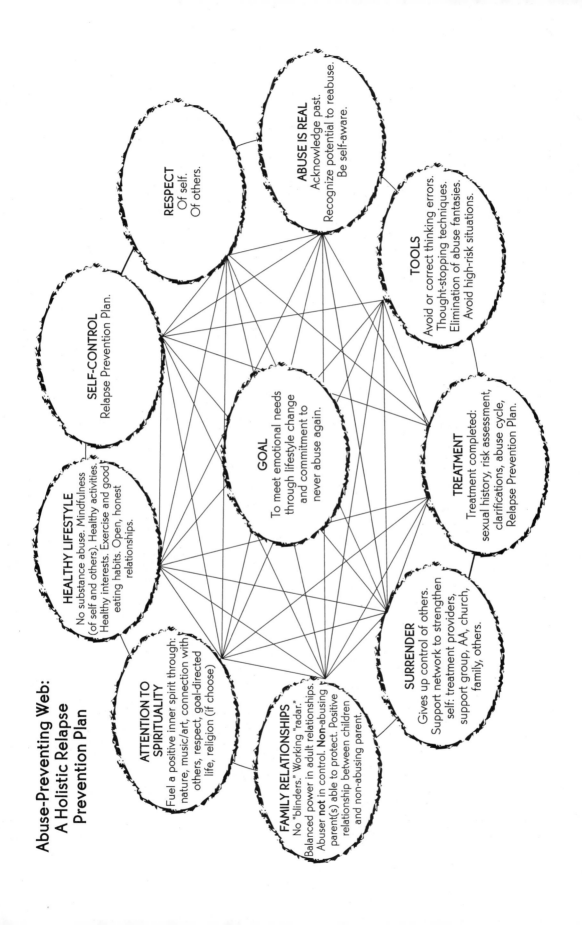

Abuse-Preventing Web:
A Holistic Relapse
Prevention Plan

RESPECT
Of self.
Of others.

ABUSE IS REAL
Acknowledge past.
Recognize potential to reabuse.
Be self-aware.

TOOLS
Avoid or correct thinking errors.
Thought-stopping techniques.
Elimination of abuse fantasies.
Avoid high-risk situations.

SELF-CONTROL
Relapse Prevention Plan.

GOAL
To meet emotional needs
through lifestyle change
and commitment to
never abuse again.

TREATMENT
Treatment completed:
sexual history, risk assessment,
clarifications, abuse cycle,
Relapse Prevention Plan.

HEALTHY LIFESTYLE
No substance abuse. Mindfulness
(of self and others). Healthy activities.
Healthy interests. Exercise and good
eating habits. Open, honest
relationships.

SURRENDER
Gives up control of others.
Support network to strengthen
self: treatment providers,
support group, AA, church,
family, others.

ATTENTION TO
SPIRITUALITY
Fuel a positive inner spirit through:
nature, music/art, connection with
others, respect, goal-directed
life, religion (if choose)

FAMILY RELATIONSHIPS
No "blinders." Working "radar."
Balanced power in adult relationships.
Abuser not in control. Non-abusing
parent(s) able to protect. Positive
relationship between children
and non-abusing parent.

each other part. "Respect for others," for example, leads to "admitting abuse" and developing empathy, as well as to "*self*-control" instead of control of others. "Completing treatment" and developing a "healthy lifestyle" feed into developing a strong sense of "spirituality." The abuse-*preventing* web also shows how changes in the "family relationship dynamics" can strengthen the family, increase safety for children, and hold the abuser responsible for sticking to the relapse prevention plan. The corners of the relapse prevention web are visible, open, and connected to newer, healthier parts of the abuser's abuse-free lifestyle.

Clarification and Restitution

If the person who abused a child in your situation wants to try to repair the emotional and psychological harm, that person must admit responsibility and apologize to *everyone* he or she has hurt. What good do apologies do? Can a bunch of words really take away emotional pain?

Language, the use of words, is one of the most basic ways we communicate. Abusers use words to communicate with their victims and with their families. Abusers use words in forming their thinking errors and developing their abuse cycles. Remember that thinking errors are thoughts that twist words around the facts in order to control others and avoid personal responsibility. These thoughts become the words that sexual abusers use to trick, confuse, control, and blame. But words can heal as well as hurt. Words are part of apologies, but that is not where abusers must start in repairing injury to others.

If you are the abusing person and have deeply violated the trust of others, your first task is to earn the *opportunity* to regain the trust of your family and of society as a whole. This opportunity is not something families or society *owe* to sexual abusers: it comes only to those who work hard in treatment. People who abuse must prove that they understand their own behavior and that they are changing the way they operate in the world.

The abuser's first step in regaining trust is admitting wrongdoing and taking pressure off the abused child and off the family. By admitting what they have done, abusers demonstrate the capacity to put a child's need to be believed and supported ahead of their own need to protect themselves through denial. This admission also puts the family's need to protect children above the abuser's need to be in control. Taking on the legal burden of responsibility for his or her own behavior shows that the abuser recognizes that the child is an innocent victim and should be spared the emotionally painful process of testifying in court.

Full admission of responsibility is one of the first signs that an abuser has the capacity for empathy and change and, therefore, may benefit from treatment. Admitting the abuse helps abusers earn the right to enter treatment, but it does not guarantee successful treatment. Once in treatment, abusers can work to demonstrate their ability to change from a lifestyle of lies and manipulations to a lifestyle of honesty and respect for others. For some abusers, this change will be impossible. For others — those who want to see themselves as caring, loving members of a family and of society — this change may be possible.

After admitting their abusive behavior, abusers should use words to reveal in detail how they took advantage of the abused child's trust and of the family's need to rely on the abuser. Abusers must show that they are aware of all the ways they controlled and hurt the child and the family. Only after they gain this awareness can they truly apologize for what they have done and work to repair the harm through a process called *restitution*.[8]

Restitution is more than saying, "I'm sorry." Restitution means to restore, to give back, to *do* something that repairs the injury to others. Restitution involves action, not simply remorse and apologies. What can abusers do to repair injury? That is a good question. The abuser cannot "take back" the abusive actions or take away all the ways the abuse affected the child. But by taking responsibility for the abuse and by clarifying what happened to the child and to the family, the abuser can remove some of the mystery and confusion around the abuse. Often this can prevent a child from developing trauma bonds or, if they have already developed, help remove those bonds.

There are other, more concrete things abusers can do to help restore their families. For example, when the abuser is an adult with income, paying for the child's and family's treatment is one restorative step. When the abuser is an older child, making a contribution from an allowance, a paper route, or a part-time job or even by collecting returnable bottles can be a restorative step. A therapist can help family members and abusers think about what other kinds of restitution would be helpful.

Throughout this book we have looked at how child sexual abuse causes hidden emotional and psychological injury to children. Much of this injury occurs when children are manipulated by the abuser or confused by the turmoil after disclosure into believing that they are to blame for "letting" the abuse happen. Clearly it's not the child's fault for thinking this way. During their abuse, children are left to sort through their confusion by themselves and draw their own conclusions. In fact, when they're young, most children think they're responsible for everything. We see this frequently in divorce cases when children think they are to blame for their parents' unhappiness and inability to stay together. This perception does not occur because the parents *tell* them they're to blame; this perception occurs because children *feel* the tension, the emotional withdrawal by a parent during times of high stress, and the frequent parental conflict over the children. Abusers often take advantage of children's tendency to see themselves as the cause of problems and use this developmental fact to persuade a child that he or she is partially or totally responsible for the abuse. Because of the abuser's manipulations, some children are never able to tell anyone about their abuser.

Despite overwhelming pressure to keep silent, however, other abused children's sense that something is wrong prompts them to disclose the secret abuse to someone. In the rare instance when disclosure comes from someone other than the abused child, the family's naturally upset reactions only magnify the child's sense of just how wrong the situation was. Not all victimized children have adults who believe and support them from the moment of disclosure. When the reaction includes anger and blaming the child, it is no wonder the abused child may begin to question, "How could I have let it happen? I'm just as much to blame. I didn't even scream."

This can be particularly confusing for children whose abuse starts when they are very young, before they begin to have any understanding of what sexual behavior really is. The abuser may have presented it as a silly secret game they could play together. Abused children's perceptions shift dramatically when they begin their own sexual development as teenagers and become painfully aware of the unacceptability of sexual contact with a relative. The potential for shame and self-blame increases dramatically during this developmental stage. These children, with no clear memories of how the abuse began, may think that they willingly participated in the abuse.

Considering that sexual abusers steal respect, trust, innocence, self-confidence, and choice from children and their families, it becomes clear that part of repairing the hidden emotional and psychological pain must include restitution—giving something back to the child who was abused and to the family. Just as the abuser used words to control and abuse others, so the abuser can use words and actions to:

- Replace tricks with truths
- Replace confusion with clearness about what happened and who is responsible
- Replace control with respect and equality
- Replace fear and threats with a sense of safety
- Replace shame and blame with self-respect

To be really effective, therefore, the abuser has to make apologies in such a way that the abused child and all family members clearly understand that the abuser accepts full responsibility for the abusive behavior. These apologies must include explanations for what occurred that are so clear that the abused child and any other children can recognize and understand the hidden ways they were controlled. Apologies that include clear explanations are called "clarifications." Jan Hindman describes in detail all the ingredients that make up a good clarification in her books *Just Before Dawn* (1989) and *The Mourning Breaks* (1991).

By clarifying how they manipulated their victims, abusers can help the children who were abused and their family understand that the children did not cause their own abuse. Knowing the details of the abuser's manipulations can help children and nonabusing parents be aware of abusive patterns of behavior and be better able to protect themselves in the future. Remember that when a magician explains his tricks, the tricks lose their power to fool and control the audience. In the same way, clarifications can change and repair the way a person sees reality and feels about himself or herself. When abusers explain the abuse, they lose some of their power to manipulate and control. When abusers accept full responsibility, they can take some of the shame and all of the blame off the children who were abused.

Becoming completely truthful, building empathy for others, taking responsibility, and recognizing the harmful effects of sexual abuse can take a sexual abuser a lot of work and a great deal of time. Abused children often have to wait months or even years before they actually hear their abusers take responsibility, deliver their full clarifications of what they did, and apologize. This waiting can be particularly harmful if the abuser denied his or her behavior and blamed the abused child at the time of the disclosure.

This denial, fairly common in the beginning, often comes from fear of consequences and anger at being exposed. Many abusers do drop their denial and admit the abuse within days or weeks after the disclosure. Because of the protective no-contact rule between children and their abusers, however, most abused children and their siblings never get to hear this early admission by the abuser. What often remains for months in the children's minds are the denying and blaming statements made by the abuser before he or she left home or before the abused child was removed by a protective services worker. When family members feel loyalty to the abuser, they often believe these early statements and take on the abuser's first way of reacting: denying and blaming the child.

When it is safe and in the best interest of the child and the family, some treatment programs try to correct this waiting problem through an early intervention with the family. In this kind of intervention, the abuser meets in one or more therapy sessions with the nonabusing parents, the abused child, and the other children in the family to explain what he or she did to hurt the abused child and the family. The abuser makes a sincere apology for causing such emotional pain in the hearts — the spritiual cores — of everyone in the family.[9] Although this early apology does not provide full restitution, it begins to reduce any potential family pressure on the child who was abused and helps siblings get rid of their confusion about what happened and who is responsible.

This early apology allows family members to reconsider their loyalty to the abusing person and to support the child who was abused. It also allows abused children who might feel responsible for and worried about the abuser to see him or her in person and to realize that the abuser is alive and okay. This is important for children who may feel that their disclosure destroyed the abuser. Because abusers are not ready at this stage to identify and explain all their ways of manipulating and hurting, they must continue their work in individual sessions and group sessions with other abusers.

Through apologies and clarifications, nonabusing parents and other family members also can play an important part in reducing emotional pain. In some situations, no one in the family knew about the abuse, and they had no way to protect the children. But in other situations, the nonabusing parents could have done something differently to protect the child. If they can figure that out, nonabusing parents can explain it and help restore the children's confidence that their parents will be able to keep them safe in the future. Nonabusing family adults might want to give the abused child and siblings their own clarifications, including explanations and apologies, for not keeping them safe, for wearing blinders, or for not realizing that their radar wasn't working. Sometimes family members might want to apologize for not believing the child in the first place, or for blaming the child for causing the abuse.

Family members can help repair damage to children's self-esteem by believing them, supporting them, and letting them know that the abuse was not their fault. Family members can play an important part in how child-victims see themselves after the abuse is over. Does the child regain a sense of pride, or does the shame continue? Does the feeling of being different or separate from the rest of the family ever go away? A lot depends on how much support the family gives to the child who was abused and to the other children.

Notes

1. Murphy, W. D., & Smith, T. A. (1996). Sex offenders against children: Empirical and clinical issues. In J. Briere, L. Berliner, J.A. Bulkley, C. Jenny, & T. Reid (Eds.),

The *APSAC handbook on child maltreatment* (pp. 175–191). Thousand Oaks, Calif.: Sage.

2. Hindman, J. (1989). *Just before dawn*. Ontario, Ore.: AlexAndria Associates.

3. Hindman, J. (1989). *Just before dawn*. Ontario, Ore.: AlexAndria Associates.

4. Murphy, W. D., & Smith, T. A. (1996). Sex offenders against children: Empirical and clinical issues. In J. Briere, L. Berliner, J.A. Bulkley, C. Jenny, & T. Reid (Eds.), *The APSAC handbook on child maltreatment* (pp. 175–191). Thousand Oaks, Calif.: Sage.

5. Adapted from Isaac, C. (1993). Training seminar on youthful abusers. Augusta, Maine.

6. Pithers, W. D., Kashima, K., Cumming, G., Beal, L., & Buell, M. (1988). Relapse prevention of sexual aggression. In R. A. Prentky & V. I. Quinsey (Eds.), *Human sexual aggression: Current perspectives*. New York: New York Academy of Sciences.

7. Gilgun, J. (1994). Avengers, conquerors, playmates, and lovers: Roles played by child sexual abuse perpetrators. *Families in Society: The Journal of Contemporary Human Services* 10, 467–480.

8. Hindman, J. (1989). *Just before dawn*. Ontario, Ore.: AlexAndria Associates.

9. Madanes, C. (1995, February). Training seminar on interventions in abusive relationships. Miami, Fla.

20

Surviving Treatment: Coping with Painful Emotions

Sexual abuse treatment is *not* easy. It is emotionally painful to face a hurtful truth. You and members of your family may feel differently at different times — sometimes seeing the issues clearly, but at other times slipping back into old ways of thinking about the problem. The abuser may be out of the home, staying in a rented room or placed in foster care or a group home. For some members of your family, this may be a relief, while for others, it may be especially difficult. Such separation can cause financial and emotional burdens. When the abuser is a parent, the other parent often feels a deep frustration and resentment at being left alone to cope with all the child care. Sometimes families blame the child who was abused for telling someone outside the family. For the abused child, the relief of having the abuse finally stop is often replaced by deep sadness at being removed from the home or by enormous guilt because the abuser is not home.

The healing process requires finding ways to tolerate painful feelings associated with facing problems, while at the same time holding on to hopeful feelings associated with discovering solutions. If people can tolerate emotional pain, they will not have to hide or run away from problems that cause pain. Family members of abused child ren will be able to support the steps necessary to the child's healing from hidden emotional injuries. Family members of abusers will be able to support the hard steps necessary to the abuser's control of abusive behaviors.

It is natural for family members to feel overwhelmed with sadness and anger by the challenge of facing and solving the problems of sexual abuse. Family members may express these feelings openly or they may keep their feelings inside, turning their anger inward in the form of depression.

When people feel unable to control these inward-directed feelings, the depression becomes deeper. Unhappy events and troubling thoughts whirl around in an ever-tightening circle, pulling them down into a hopeless, powerless place inside themselves. Hopelessness can lead to thoughts and talk of *suicide*. Suicidal talk should always be listened to and evaluated by professionals to learn whether the individual has serious intentions and a plan for self-harm. With the help of counseling and family support, suicidal individuals can find ways to help themselves and others and see hope for the future. Suicidal talk can mean different things with different people.

When adult sexual abusers talk about suicide, they may be overwhelmed with feelings of shame and guilt. They may feel terrible about what they have done. But even so, when sexual abusers talk about suicide, they are continuing their pattern of putting their own needs first and not thinking about what is best for the abused child or the family. They are not thinking about the past and present harm they have already caused and their responsibility for repairing some of that harm. They are not thinking about the harm that their real or threatened suicide would cause the abused child and the family in the future.

When adult abusers talk of depression and suicide, they make their own emotional pain more important than their victim's pain. Family members often stop worrying about what has happened to the abused child (which appears to be only in the past) and begin thinking only about the abuser's pain and their fear of the abuser's possible suicide attempt. Suicidal talk by adult sexual abusers can be just one more thinking error the abuser is using to control the way others respond to him or her. Sexual abusers often manipulate others into worrying more about them than about anyone else.

Adolescents who sexually abuse younger children may also feel suicidal at times. Although they may feel terrible about what they've done, they may have the same self-serving motives as adult abusers. Adolescents may lack sufficient life experience in developing solutions, so they may truly doubt their own ability to face their problems. Parents and family members need to be particularly involved and connected with these adolescents so that they don't give up before they've had a chance in treatment to learn how to control their behavior and to develop confidence in their ability to change.

Nonabusing parents also may feel suicidal: they may feel betrayed by the abuser; worried about the abused or the abusing child, or both; ashamed in their community; overwhelmed with the stress of parenting and the financial strain; and often angry with themselves for not knowing about or preventing the abuse. They may be afraid of the family falling apart and doubt their own ability to cope with the situation. When they feel that life will never get better, it is understandable that they feel like giving up. But if nonabusing parents give in to these thoughts, they are not remembering their responsibility to do what is best for their children: to get stronger and help their children get through this stressful time in their lives.

Abused and abusing children need adults — both nonabusing parents and abusers — who can put aside the desire to escape from a painful, embarrassing, and shameful situation. Abused and abusing children need adults who can recognize and work to repair the harm the children have suffered. *Abused* children need parents and other adults to take care of them and protect them. *Abusing* children need parents and other adults to care for them and hold them responsible for changing their abusive behavior patterns.

Suicide is not a fair choice for parents: their job as parents is not over. Their job is to provide a safe, loving environment where their children can grow. Their job is to help their children grow into healthy, confident, loved people who feel good about themselves, good about their bodies, and good about their normal sexuality.

Children who have been abused, or who have been witnesses to abuse, might also suffer significant depression. Children may feel responsible for causing the abuse and the postdisclosure family pain, even though it is not their fault. Children may think about suicide because they can't see a way out of feeling bad and sad. They may feel hopeless and powerless. They may believe that life will never change, never get any better, that they will never be loved or happy again.

Children need help moving through these feelings and beliefs. They need to know that they are believed, loved, and supported. They need to be told by the abuser, by the nonabusing parents, and by everyone around them that the sexual abuse was not their fault. Children need to understand how the abuser made them victims in the abuse. Children need to believe that life will improve, that others feel good about them, and that they have the power to make changes in the way they feel about themselves.

Getting out of the whirlpool of reactive emotions is not easy and cannot be done all at once. It happens one step at a time. Sometimes the step consists of talking about the feelings, and sometimes the step is simply doing something different to get outside of the whirling current of emotions. Often it means reaching out to someone for help in the fight against depression.

Fighting a whirlpool of emotions is a bit like fighting a whirlpool in the ocean. Imagine that your boat has capsized in the middle of a strong current and that you are being pulled closer and closer into a strong whirlpool. Eventually, the whirlpool draws you into its downward spiral, and you are being pulled under the surface of the water. You have a choice at this point — you can do nothing, or you can fight the current and call out for help. If you just let your arms and legs hang down close to your body, and you do not fight the current, eventually you will end up on the bottom, where no one can stay alive for long. But if you use your arms to stroke and your legs to kick, you can pull yourself out of the downward spiral. You can fight to get back to the top before too much water builds up over your head. If you look around for help, there may be someone or something nearby to grab onto, so you do not have to struggle so hard by yourself. If you fight the pull of the whirlpool and get support and help from others, you can reach safety.

Like fighting the whirlpool in the ocean, it is never easy to fight the whirlpool of depression, but counseling sessions can help you find ways to begin. Some beginning steps could be:

- Recognizing that being depressed about some things does not mean that your whole life is hopeless.
- Not thinking painful thoughts over and over.
- Increasing the use and strength of the thinking part of your brain, which knows that the emotional part of your brain can't see things clearly right now.
- Using these thoughts to take control over your emotions.
- Making choices for yourself; not letting your emotions hide your ability to change things.
- Doing something positive to change one part of a depressing situation.

If you are the one who sexually abused a child:

- Get your thoughts and behaviors under control.
- Develop pride in taking responsibility for the abuse onto yourself and off the child.
- Remember that there are things you can still do to repair harm to the child.

If you are the nonabusing parent:

- Learn how you can help your child and feel better about yourself, about your family, and about your life.

- Remember that by taking responsibility for yourself, by learning what you need to do to become a more supportive, protective parent, you can change the way you are feeling.
- Take responsibility for yourself.

If you are the child who was abused or a sibling in the family:

- Remember that you are a child, and you are not responsible for your own abuse or for the unhappiness in your family.
- Write a list of all the positive things about yourself or about your life.
- Write a list of all the things you want to do with your life.

Tell yourself that things will get better when you understand the situation better and when the adults and older people around you learn how to take responsibility for themselves and their behavior.

part five

Remain Separate or Reunify:
Making the Best Decision for Your Family

21

....

Should Your Family Get Back Together?

When family members have been separated to protect some members from the abusive actions of other members, many important things must be considered when trying to decide whether your family should get back together. Reuniting your family is not a goal of treatment. The main goal of treatment is to help your family members—all of you—to heal and grow in ways that will prevent this kind of abuse from happening again. At some point in your treatment you will need to make a decision about whether future contact with the abuser is in the best interest of the children in your family, and your therapy will help you weigh all the factors. For many families, successful treatment means choosing to have no contact with the abuser in order to protect the emotional health and/or physical safety of all family members. For other families, supervised contact makes the most sense. And for still other families, a decision to have the family live together again makes sense based on the children's needs, the nonabusing parent's ability to provide protection, and the abuser's progress in treatment. First let's look at why family members are apart, and then we'll look at what they need to accomplish before it makes sense to even consider family reunification.

The most common response by protective services agencies to the disclosure of child sexual abuse is to require no contact between the alleged abuser and the child who was abused and any other children who might be at risk. Usually it is the abuser who moves out, but this is not always the case. Sometimes a youthful or adolescent abuser is allowed to stay home while getting treatment. This should happen only when professionals have determined that the abusing child is under control and that a family is able to provide supervision and safety for the victim. But sometimes it happens simply because there is no other place for the child or adolescent to go. For all adult abusers and most adolescents, however, the early protective decision is usually for the abuser to live outside of the home during the first stages of treatment. Often, the adult abuser was already living outside the home during the abuse. This might happen in cases of divorce or when the abuser is a relative outside the immediate family, such as an uncle or aunt, cousin, or grandparent.

Sometimes it is the abused child who moves, or is placed, out of the home. Difficult as it may be for the child and for the family, sometimes moving the abused child into a safer living situation away from the home is the best option available. For some children, this may be a permanent move. But in many situations, the move is temporary, allowing family members time to recover from the shock of the disclosure and to gain the strength needed to face the problem of abuse. Nonabusing parents usually miss their children and worry about them when they are not home. These parents work very hard in treatment to make the changes necessary for their children to return home.

Specialists who understand what you are going through can help you make a decision about reunification. With counseling and your own hard work, you can develop a better understanding of what changes are needed in your family to prevent sexual abuse from happening again. Your new understanding and a positive attitude about treatment can help move things along in a positive direction. After some time in treatment, the counselors can help you evaluate whether your family has changed enough to keep your children safe.

When Does Family Reunification Make Sense?

Many families think that separating the abuser from the abused child is always a temporary arrangement. When families are hoping for reunification, family members are concerned about how long they will be separated and how soon they can get back together.

There are two basic levels of reunification: at one level, the abuser and the abused child see each other under the protective supervision of another approved adult, but they do not live in the same home; at the second level, the abuser returns to live in the same home with the abused child and/or other children and the nonabusing parents. Whether or not your family reunifies will be one of your family's most important decisions, made with the help of trained professionals: protective workers, social workers or other specialized therapists, even probation officers or judges.

Basically, reunification depends on the treatment progress you and your family — including the abuser — make.[1] No treatment is exactly the same for all families. However, there are some basic steps that must be accomplished before a family should consider living with the abuser.

Reunification makes sense only if the abuser and the family can be sure that he or she will never touch children sexually again. The abuser must understand his or her problem behavior, take responsibility for it, offer restitution through clarifications and apologies to the abused child and family, and develop a relapse prevention plan that includes who to call for help when those urges to manipulate and abuse power return — and they will return. It's not the absence of urges but what the abuser chooses to do about those urges that indicates treatment progress.

Reunification makes sense only if the children trust that the nonabusing adults in the family can support them, empathize with them, and know enough about the problem to keep them safe. The protecting adults must fully understand the abuser's problem, including the secret web of control and manipulation. Equally important, nonabusing adults must understand if and how their own personal qualities or conditions might have kept them from being protective in the past. Nonabusing adults must be able to change those conditions to reassure the children that they will be able to protect them. A nonabusing adult should be able to communicate directly and to effectively confront the abuser about thinking errors or manipulations. She or he must be able to take action to report any renewal of inappropriate touching and to limit or eliminate the abuser's access to the children.

Reunification makes sense only when, and if, the victim and other children feel confident that the nonabusing parent can protect them, and only if the children want the abuser back in the home. No child or family member should ever have full trust in the abuser. Sexual abuse of children is the kind of problem behavior that the abuser will have to work to control for the rest of his or her life. Abusers must share their individual abuse cycles and their personal relapse prevention plans with their families. This information will help family members be aware of any warning signs if the abuser should take a step toward abusing again. Sometimes it just isn't safe for abusers to live with their families again. Sometimes children who have been abused and family members, understandably, do not want to be with the abuser again.

Note

1. Meinig, M. B., & Bonner, B. L. (1990). Returning the treated sex offender to the family. *Violence Update*, 1, 1–11.

22

....

Less than the Whole Truth:
Conditions that Make Family Reunification Unsafe

You have spent a lot of time, at this point, trying to understand the whole problem of sexual abuse in families. Now is a good time to once again stress the importance of knowing all the facts — the truth — which is key to helping abused children, families, and abusers heal and grow with less pain and shame about the abuse.

We have already looked at the importance of telling the truth, but it is one of the most difficult tasks to accomplish. Sometimes there seems to be no one truth; everyone in the family sees the situation differently. Or some "facts" seem to rule out other "facts." While there are indeed many viewpoints, when we talk here about the "truth," we are referring to certain facts about the sexual abuse: who, what, when, where, how. In the courts, "truth" is about trying to determine the facts of a case and the honesty of a speaker. Because child sexual abuse is a behavior that is treated both in the court system and in a therapeutic environment, it is important to include language about "truth" in treatment.

The truth is difficult, because it can sometimes be the source of shame, embarrassment, and emotional pain for family members. Sometimes, people can accept hearing about some things but not about others. Sometimes the abuser can admit to part of the sexual behavior but not all of it. Sometimes everyone is afraid that individuals or the family will fall apart if it all comes out. So, sometimes family members want to tell or hear just enough of the truth to get the abuse to stop. Sometimes family members are afraid that if more truth comes out, treatment will take longer and the abuser will be kept away from home longer. Perhaps the abuser might have to go to court again as more truth is told. Often family members are afraid to tell all the truth if it means that everyone in the family will be angry or blame them for being honest.

There is a serious problem, however, if some of the truth stays hidden. The problem is that abused children, siblings, abusers, and nonabusing parents could leave treatment while the ingredients and patterns of sexual abuse are still in place in their family. Remember that it is not just sexual touching or exposure that is involved but also secrecy, manipulation and control of others, thinking errors, fear of consequences, shame, protection of others, and minimization and denial of the problem.

Recall the earlier example of removing a splinter from under the skin's surface. Remember that infection can grow and spread if the entire splinter and all its tiny fragments are not removed. Sexual abuse is like an infected wound in the family. If all the ingredients of sexual abuse are not removed, they can sit there quietly invisible for a while, but the infection continues to fester and grow, eventually spreading throughout the whole family. Although your family may appear to have changed and the members look ready to get back together, there may still be secret "splinters" of abuse that your therapists won't know about until someone tells them. So, the responsibility is on the abuser and the protective parent to be totally honest. Otherwise, the risk of sexual abuse happening again in the family is very high. Let's look a little closer at some conditions that would not support family reunification, even if lots of other positive changes have already been made.

Abusers are not safe to rejoin the family whenever they:

- Cover up the truth, control others, and minimize their problem behavior.
- Hide pieces of truth and, thus, learn that they can still manipulate others and "get away" with something they have done.
- Fool themselves into believing that they are safe because even though they have secret sexual thoughts, they are not acting out sexually at the time. Secret thoughts about sexually abusive actions always come before the sexually abusive behavior. It is only a matter of time before the secret thoughts become more powerful and move an abuser toward acting on those thoughts.
- Do not take responsibility for and apologize for *all* the abuse. Instead of fully repairing the hurt inside the abused child, the abuser is covering the truth to protect himself or herself. This is the same way of thinking that exists in sexual abusers' minds at the time of the abuse: abusers think of what they want for themselves, not what's best for the child.
- Continue to feel shame because of continued manipulative and dishonest behavior in treatment. Bad feelings about oneself are usually part of the feelings that can start an abuser's cycle of abusive behavior.
- Say one thing (that they love their family and would never abuse again) while holding on to those old patterns of manipulative thinking that can lead them to sexually abuse again.
- Do not know their abuse cycle or have not developed a relapse prevention plan.

If abusers stay in a pattern of controlling the family and do not take responsibility for telling the whole truth, then abused children may become stuck in confusing, no-win situations, unsure whether to tell everything.

Abused children and siblings are not safe from abuse whenever they:

- Are not clear in their own minds that they are the victims.

- Still believe they are to blame for the abuse and still feel some responsibility to protect the abuser.

- Feel forced to become a "team" with the abuser, continuing to keep some secrets from the rest of the family and from the treatment providers. In an unspoken agreement to keep silent, the child may feel pressured not to betray the abuser's lack of complete honesty about the abuse. For example, the abuser may admit that the abuse happened a couple of times or admit fondling the child but not admit that the abuse occurred over several years or that it included more invasive sexual abuse such as digital penetration or intercourse. Just as in the original abuse, the abuser and the child again "share a secret." The abuser stays in control. This puts the child in the same powerless position as before treatment started: protecting the abuser and keeping the nonabusing parent from knowing the truth.

- Use unhealthy thinking patterns — minimization and denial — that were going on during the abuse. Instead of feeling free to tell the whole truth, the child may go back to old ways of burying the truth: "It's no big deal. The abuser told *most* of the truth." These children may not understand how they have been violated, or they may feel the need to protect the abuser from being fully responsible for the abuse. This need to protect the abuser may keep the abused child emotionally and psychologically dependent on the abuser. These abused children may continue to be controlled or hurt by memories of the abuse. They may try to reduce the feelings of powerlessness brought on by the abuse and the abuse memories by taking on the behaviors of the abuser and acting out sexually with younger children. That is why having professional help is so important in helping children recover from the effects of their abuse.

- Do not feel supported to give up the old patterns of powerlessness and protection of others that they learned to cope with the abuse. Without help to change these patterns, children may carry them outside the family and minimize abusive behavior in others. Abused children and siblings, therefore, may be at risk for future abuse by others.

Nonabusing spouses, parents, and caretakers cannot keep children safe whenever they:

- Do not understand all the ways the abuser manipulates and controls.
- Do not know the abuser's abuse cycle and relapse prevention plan.
- Do not understand all the ways the abused child has been affected, and possibly traumatized, by the abuse.
- Do not understand all the ways other children in the family may have been hurt, and possibly traumatized, by the abuse.
- Are not willing to look at *whether* and *how* they may have played a part in a making a family atmosphere in which one family member could abuse another.
- Are not prepared to make needed changes to keep children safe in the future.
- Feel more supportive of the abuser than they do of the abused child.
- Continue to blame the abused child for the abuse happening or for the consequences of disclosure.
- Continue to hold the abused child responsible for not telling sooner.
- Are not able to recognize warning signs of the abuser taking control.
- Are not able to recognize warning signs inside themselves that they are giving up control and feeling manipulated or powerless.

When abusers are not able to care enough about their victims to take full responsibility for the abuse and to make efforts toward restitution for all the harm they caused, they are called *untreated abusers.* Although they may have gone through many of the steps of treatment and may seem to have changed a lot, they still have not learned enough to know how to stop their abusive behaviors. They have not changed enough to be safe around children. Doing treatment partway does not work. This makes sense when you think of treatment for other kinds of problems.

Let's say you had a bad ear infection, for example. The doctor would give you some antibiotic medicine and tell you that you must take it for *all 10* days. You probably know what would happen if you stopped taking the medicine after only five or six days. Even though you were feeling better, and even though you looked better to others, your treatment would not work completely. After a few days, the infection would come back. When an infection comes back, sometimes it is stronger than the first time, because the body is worn out trying to fight off the infection. If treatment is to be successful—if all the hard work you and your family are putting into treatment is really going to make long-lasting changes in family patterns—then the whole truth has to come out. All parts of the abusive patterns must change during treatment.

23

Looking for the End of Treatment: It's a Long and Winding Road

There is nothing quick or easy about treatment. It takes a lot of hard work to get through everything and make permanent changes. That doesn't mean there isn't progress along the way. Anyone who works hard will make progress and learn a lot. But if changes are going to last—if you are going to reach your final goal of being safe and have pride in yourself for accomplishing these goals—you have to go through all the stages of treatment.

Going all the way in treatment is like climbing a mountain. Imagine that you and your family choose a mountain where you've heard that the climb is somewhat difficult. You've also heard that there will be clear trails and glimpses of views along the way, with the reward of the most spectacular view of the whole valley from the top. At first, you doubt that you can reach the top of such a steep mountain, but you have a guide who can point you in the right direction. You start slowly, but as you take one step at a time and become familiar with the trail, you gain confidence, and having a guide helps. When you reach difficult spots along the trail, family members help one another with encouraging cheers of "You can do it!" Your muscles ache and your breathing is difficult at times, but after a while, someone ahead yells back to the others, "Come on! There's a bit of a view from here." You reach the spot, and indeed it is a fine view. You look down into the valley and marvel at how far you've come.

After you rest a while, your guide suggests moving on. But thoughts of climbing more are not welcome, and you try to convince the others that you've all come far enough, that the view from the top won't be that much better. But someone else speaks out, "Oh, but this view here is only a small part of what we'll be able to see from the top. From this side of the mountain we can see in only one direction. But from the top, we'll be able to see all parts of the valley and many other mountain peaks. We'll be able to see in all directions." Then you try to convince the others to go ahead, that you'll wait for them to come back down. But your family refuses to accept that, and someone says, "If we are all going to share the experience, we must all work together to get to the top. Those who don't get to the top won't know what the rest of us are seeing. Come on, let me help you up through this next difficult section."

When family members work together to reach the top, they will all share the same view, and the hardest part of the climb will be over. That doesn't mean that coming down the mountain will be easy, as your muscles will be weary, and you will need to walk with care so as not to slip and fall. But you will have accomplished what you set out to do. You may pick a different trail or come down over the same trail. In either case, you are now an experienced hiker, and you will be wiser and have an easier time on the way back down. So each family member must decide how far to climb and how much to work together to reach the same goal.

So it is in treatment. There is often a slow start and uncertainty about the goals, but as family members gain confidence in their own steps, they begin to work together to encourage and help one another through difficult spots. When you're partway through the treatment process, it may feel that you've been through enough and that you see a "view" that you couldn't see before the disclosure. It is not uncommon to want to stop and put the abuse behind you. You understand much more than before, and you're sure that this new insight will keep your family safe in the future. And it is true that you have learned a lot and can see more than before disclosure and treatment. But stopping partway through treatment means that although you have learned some things and made some changes, you will *not* have finished all there is to do.

Stopping midway, before you have gone through the hardest part of treatment, often means that the changes do not become permanent, that you did not work at it long enough to get to the point where things become easier. Going through all the steps in treatment, however, means that you and your family have worked together and share the same clear vision about how you want your family to be.

Just as it is okay to rest along the way when climbing a mountain, so it is fine for victims and survivors, both children and adults, to take an occasional break from treatment. Because children understand things differently at different ages, it makes sense to go as far in treatment as possible at one age and then come back for more counseling at a later age. Although it's important for nonabusing parents to stay in treatment long enough to learn all the ways to support and protect their children, sometimes nonabusing parents have memories of their own abuse during childhood that are difficult to face all at once. Often what seems clear at one time becomes confused at another time. So it's important to think of treatment as something you can come back to anytime it makes sense.

It is *never* a good idea, however, for sexual abusers to take a break from treatment. Taking a break means not learning all the steps it takes to stop abusive behavior.

Hope for Change and Healing

It is difficult to know how the sexual abuse will affect each member of your family now or years in the future. Every person and every situation are unique. The amount of long-lasting emotional harm, both visible and hidden, that each family member experiences depends partly on what the abuser has done, partly on the abuser's efforts to repair that harm, but mostly on the amount of support each person receives from other family members.

Even when abusers do not take responsibility for the harm they have caused, abused children and other family members can recover from the effects of sexual abuse. Many abused children and their families are strong and clear in their thinking about what happened. Many families and children have a strong quality of *resilience*, the ability to bounce back from trauma or harm and go on in their lives. How well children deal with the rest of their lives depends in part on how much support and understanding the family gives to the abused child and siblings once they become aware of the abuse. Many families are able to help children learn that sexual abuse is not their fault. Many families are able to help siblings understand how confusion and fear might have made them feel powerless during the abuse situation.

Each child and each family are different. Each situation presents an opportunity for hope and change. It will not be easy work, but it can be work that makes a real difference in each family member's life. Abusers have used their ways of thinking and manipulating for much of their lifetimes, so they will have to work hard to change the thoughts and feelings that lead to abusive behavior. Abusers must realize that they will have to spend the rest of their lives watching for any signs that their abusive behavior could be returning. Families also must learn to recognize all the controlling signs of abusive behavior if they show up again or if they exist in other relationships.

Many families have been successful in doing this hard work of learning all the ways to protect their children and making decisions about how much contact to have with the abuser. For some families, this hard work brings them to a strong protective decision not to have the abuser return home or not to have further contact with the abuser. Choosing not to reunify is not a failure of treatment. Choosing not to reunify can be based on the best estimation of how to help the children and the nonabusing adults heal and how to keep the children safe.

Even when a clear decision has been made, it will not be easy. If the abuser is one of the parents, child custody and visitation issues may arise when the decision is not to reunite. Getting the best legal and therapeutic advice you can will help you keep the children safe.

In families where members choose to keep the abuser a part of their lives, however, abusers must continue to work hard *every day* to make themselves safe around children. Remember that only those abusers who are committed to their treatment can accomplish changes inside themselves. In previous chapters we looked at all the conditions that must exist before families can consider having contact with the abuser. No family can be truly safe if it allows an *untreated* sexual abuser to live in or have unsupervised visits with the family.

With or without the abuser, the other family members can get back together or continue together and get on with their lives. Some people are afraid that their families will never be the same. This is true: after a lot of hard work in treatment, your family will be changed. But this can be a good thing.

Think of how you might act if a special, beautiful vase that you have treasured all your life falls and breaks. With careful searching, you might be able to locate all the pieces, but some pieces are very damaged. You may be sad to realize that you will not be able to glue the vase back the way it was.

But as you continue to study the pieces, you develop a new vision of how the vase might look. You discard the cracked and weak pieces. Using only the brightest and strongest pieces and the right glue, you are able to put the vase back together in a mosaic pattern. It is not the same, but it is strong, interesting, and beautiful.

So it may be with you and your family. You may feel like your family has broken apart since information about the sexual abuse first became known. You may fear that your family will never be whole again. But over time and through the course of treatment, things can change. You can develop a new vision of how you can be together, still caring for one another and feeling stronger than before the disclosure. Because of all the important work you do in treatment, you can still have beautiful times together. You can discard any weak pieces, like blinders or unreliable radar, and replace them with openness, clear awareness of your family's needs, and the ability to sense control patterns. You can change the family "glue": instead of being held together with secrets, thinking errors, and manipulations, your family can be held together with openness, straight talking, direct communication, and a new radar system. With well-operating radar, you will know where to look for and take care of any possible "torpedoes" or "mines" (return of problems) in your family.

By changing from the old way to this new vision, you can develop a new story about you and your family. Your story will no longer be about a family where sexual abuse and manipulation happens. Your story can be about a family where children are safe and the emotional and physical needs of each person are respected and valued.

It is sad for children when families can't change enough to create a safe place for them. When this happens, children cannot stay home and often have to live with another family. It's much harder for these children to find the right glue to put their lives back together. But together with their therapists and their new family and lots of other helpers such as teachers and friends, these children can develop a new vision, a new story of themselves. They can strengthen their lives by keeping the bright and shiny parts and letting go of the parts of their lives that don't fit into the new story.

appendixes

appendix a

Differences in Power: Factors to Consider when Children Interact Sexually

The list below is based on information presented by Isaacs (1993).[1] It should be regarded as a place to start and not a comprehensive list.

- What is the age difference?
- What is the size difference?
- What is the difference in self-confidence?
- Is one child more assertive than the other?
- Which child has the easier time making friends? Does either child have a hard time making friends near his or her own age?
- Does one child tend to socialize with children who look up to him or her?
- Which child has more maturity, more ability to understand what is occurring during the sexual activity?
- Which child is smarter? Is one child able to take advantage because the other is not as smart or developmentally delayed?
- What is the nature of the relationship? Does one child look up to the other? Is one child in a position of authority over the other? Have the parents placed one child in charge of the other, such as an older brother or sister or a babysitter? In such a relationship, the younger child has been told to listen to and obey the older child.
- Was force, threat, or bribery involved in the sexual activity?
- Was the sexual behavior beyond what you would expect of a child that age?

Note

1. Isaacs, C. (1993). Training seminar on youthful abusers. Augusta, Maine.

appendix b

Assessment Guidelines

These assessment guidelines for abused children, other children, nonabusing parents or spouses, other family members, and abusers suggest some factors to consider and questions to answer in a family assessment. This should be considered a minimum guideline—a place to start—not an all-inclusive list.

Assessing the Abused Child

- What are the child's strengths? Skills in managing emotions and/or behaviors? Skills in coping with stress and/or problems? Skills getting along with people?
- What is the child's level of self-esteem? How well does he or she function? How responsible is he or she? In which areas of life? Home? School? Peers?
- What interests does this child have? What activities outside the home does he or she participate in?
- What was the child like (behavior, emotions, activities) before the abuse occurred? After?
- What did the abuse consist of? How did the abuse violate the child's body?
- Was there force, violence, or the use of threats?
- How old was the child? What did the abuse mean to the child at this age?
- How often did the abuse occur? How long did it go on?
- Has the abuse traumatized or harmed the child? Physically? Emotionally? Psychologically?
- Was there more to the abuse than has been disclosed?

- Does the abused child feel responsible for the abuse? Share the blame with the abuser? Does the child clearly understand that he or she was a victim?
- What was the child's relationship with the abuser like before the abuse? After?
- To what degree is the child still trapped in a *trauma bond* with the abuse and the abuser?

Assessing Other Children
(Siblings, Cousins, Neighbors, Close Friends)

- What are the child's strengths? Skills in managing emotions and/or behaviors? Skills in coping with stress and/or problems? Skills getting along with people?
- What is the child's level of self-esteem? How well does he or she function? How responsible is he or she? In which areas of life? Home? School? Peers?
- What interests does this child have? What activities outside the home does he or she participate in?
- What was the child like (behaviors, emotions, activities) before the abuse occurred? After?
- Was this child also abused? Emotionally? Physically? Psychologically? Sexually?
- Was this child witness to, or aware of, the sexual abuse?
- Did this child feel unable or frightened to reveal the secret? Why?
- Was there force, violence, or the use of threats?
- Does this child feel responsible for the abuse? Does this child understand why he or she was unable to tell?
- Did awareness of or experience with the sexual abuse traumatize or otherwise harm this child?
- Is this child trapped in any degree of *trauma bond* with the abuse or the abuser?

Assessing the Nonabusing Spouse, Parent, or Caretaker

- What are the adult's strengths? Ability to manage emotions and/or behaviors? Skills in coping with stress and/or problems? Skills in personal relationships?
- How does this adult perceive himself or herself? What is his or her level of self-esteem? Level of self-confidence? How well does he or she function? How responsible is he or she? In which areas of life? At home? At work? With peers?
- What interests does this adult have? What activities outside the home does he or she participate in?
- How does this adult perceive his or her role as parent or caretaker of the abused child? Of the other children?
- Was there a change in self-perception before and after disclosure?
- What is the adult's level of independence? Psychological? Economic?
- Does the adult have other relationships? With friends? With relatives?
- Did this adult have any awareness of the abuse? What level?
- Is the amount of power in this family balanced equally between the adults? Does one adult control the other? If so, how?
- Are there underlying factors (e.g., childhood victimization history, substance abuse) that may have contributed to nonprotection of the child?

Assessing the Family

What does the "web of secrecy" look like in the family?

- Were other family members aware? If so, to what degree? If not, why not?
- Were other family members manipulated? Controlled? Fooled? If so, how?

- What is the relationship between children and adults in this family? Respectful? Supportive? Abusive?
- Are there underlying factors that allowed the abuser to "attach" a web of secrecy and control? If so, what are they?

What is the family *response* to learning about the sexual abuse?

- Does the nonabusing parent believe and support the child who was abused?
- Do the siblings believe and support the child who was abused?
- Does the extended family of grandparents, aunts and uncles, cousins, in-laws believe and support the child who was abused?
- Do they hold the abuser responsible? If so, how?
- What is the level of uncritical support for the abuser?
- Is the family united in the way the individual members understand the abuse, or is the family divided, with some members supporting the abuser and some supporting the abused child?

Assessing the Abuser

The list below suggests questions and factors to consider during a complete family assessment. It is not intended to be a comprehensive outline of abuser assessment or treatment. For more detail on assessing abusers, see, for example, Carich and Mussack (2001).[1]

- What are his or her strengths? Ability to manage emotions and/or behaviors? Skills in coping with stress and/or problems? Skills in personal relationships? Managing leisure time?
- How does he or she perceive himself or herself? What is his or her level of self-esteem? Level of self-confidence? How well does he or she function? How responsible is he or she? In which areas of life? At home? At work? With peers?
- Was there a change in self-perception before and after disclosure?

- How does the rest of the family and the community perceive the abuser? How does this influence whether people believe the abused child or the abuser?

- What interests does the abuser have? What activities outside the home does he or she participate in?

- How does the abuser perceive his or her role as parent or caretaker of the abused child? Of the other children?

- What is the abuser's level of independence? Psychological? Economic?

- Does he or she have other relationships? With friends? With relatives?

- Do other problems exist? Low self-esteem? Poor social skills? Poor work history or poor academic performance? Abuse of alcohol or drugs?

- Does the abuser violate others' rights in other ways? Through aggression? Disrespect of privacy? Stealing?

- How did the abuser manipulate and gain control of the child? Through a feeling of being "special"? Sharing blame? Threats? Bribery?

- What did the abuse consist of? How long did it go on? How often? How widely does the abuser's account differ from the abused child's and/or the siblings' accounts?

- How did the abuser manipulate and gain control of other family members?

- Do other sexual behaviors exist? Is there pleasure in normal sexual contact, or only in "forbidden" sexual acts? What is the nature of his or her problem?

- How long has the abuser had the problem behavior?

- What are his or her sexual arousal patterns?

- What is the degree of sexual preoccupation? Does he or she use pornography?

- Where and when did the abuser learn to use abuse to control others?

- Does the abuser admit the abuse and take full responsibility?

- Are there other victims?

Assessing the Community

- How did people think about the abuser before disclosure? Did he or she have good standing in the community? Was he or she respected? Did he or she have power?
- How did people think about the abused child before disclosure? Was he or she seen as a "good" kid? A "bad" kid? A troubled kid?
- Does the community support tend more toward the victim or the abuser? What sources of information lead you to this conclusion?
- Do neighborhood children still play or associate with the abused child?

Note

1. Carich, M. S., & Mussack, S. E. (2001). *Handbook for sexual abuse assessment and treatment*. Brandon, Vt.: Safer Society Press.

about the author

··

Constance M. Ostis is a licensed clinical social worker who served for 15 years as program coordinator of the Sexual Abuse Treatment Program at the Community Counseling Center in Portand, Maine. She received her bachelor's degree from Simmons College in 1965 and her master's degree from Smith College School for Social Work in 1971. She is currently nearing completion of her doctorate in social work at Simmons College School of Social Work in Boston.

Connie has a long professional history in the field of child welfare, beginning in the Division of Child and Family Services in Boston in the mid-1960s. In the fall of 2001 she became a faculty member in the Department of Social Work at the University of Southern Maine. Connie is a locally recognized authority on the treatment of sexual abuse within families. Her humor and her clear, informal style have made her a sought-after speaker at professional training programs and for the general public. Connie's positive style has enabled many families to work toward healing and helped many therapists find a positive focus in their own work.

Connie is the mother of three grown children, Jay, Nathan, and Lauren. Harry, her husband of 34 years, has supported both her professional and her private interests, which include kayaking, hiking, skiing, reading, and time spent with friends. While the family dog, Molly, who provided company during the writing of this book, is gone, she still has a 13-year-old cat, Sam, who spends hours curled beside her at the computer. In addition, she has enjoyed the support of her siblings and their families, as well as the good fortune of having the love and support of her mother, now 84, living near her in Maine.

about safer society press

The Safer Society Press is part of The Safer Society Foundation, Inc., a 501(c)3 nonprofit agency dedicated to the prevention and treatment of sexual abuse. We publish additional books, audiocasettes, and training videos related to the treatment of sexual abuse. To receive a catalog of our complete listings, please check the box on the order form at the back of the book and mail it to the address listed or call us at (802)247-3132. For more information on the Safer Society Foundation, Inc., visit our website at www.safer society.org.

select safer society publications

Adult Relapse Prevention Workbook by Charlene Steen, Ph.D., J.D. (2001) $22.

SOS Help for Emotions: Managing Anxiety, Anger and Depression by Lynn Clark, Ph.D. (1998) $13.50

Feeling Good Again: A Workbook for Children Aged 6 and Up Who've Been Sexually Abused by Burt Wasserman (1998) $16.

Feeling Good Again Guide for Parents and Therapists by Burt Wasserman (1998) $8.

Back On Track: Boys Dealing with Sexual Abuse (for boys ages 10 and up) by Leslie Bailey Wright and Mindy Loiselle (1997) $14.

Shining Through: Pulling It Together After Sexual Abuse (for girls ages 10 and up) by Mindy Loiselle and Leslie Bailey Wright (1997) $16.

Web of Meaning: A Developmental-Contextual Approach in Sexual Abuse Treatment by Gail Ryan and Associates (1999) $22.

Difficult Connection: The Therapeutic Relationship in Sex Offender Treatment by Geral T. Blanchard (1998) $12.

Female Sexual Abusers: Three Views by Patricia Davin, Teresa Dunbar, and Julia Hislop (1999) $22.

Outside Looking In: When Someone You Love Is in Therapy by Patrice Moulton, Ph.D., and Lin Harper, Ph.D. (1999) $20.

Handbook for Sexual Abuser Assessment and Treatment edited by Mark S. Carich, Ph.D., and Steven E. Mussack, Ph.D. (2001) $28.

Sexual Abuse in America: Epidemic of the 21st Century by Robert E. Freeman Longo and Geral T. Blanchrad (1998) $20.

The Last Secret: Daughters Sexually Abused by Mothers by Bobbie Rosencrans, M.S.W. (1997) $20.

ORDER FORM

Date:_____

All books shipped via United Parcel Service.
Please include a street location for shipping
as we cannot ship to a Post Office address.

SHIPPING ADDRESS:

Name and/or Agency _____

Street Address (no PO boxes) _____

City _____ State _____ Zip _____

BILLING ADDRESS (if different from shipping address):

Address _____

City _____ State _____ Zip _____

Daytime phone (_____)_____ P.O.#_____
                                        (must be submitted)

Visa or MasterCard # _____ Exp. Date _____

Signature (for credit card order)_____

☐ Please send me a catalog.   ☐ Do not add me to your mailing list.

QTY	TITLE	UNIT PRICE	TOTAL COST

SUBTOTAL	
VT RESIDENTS ADD 5% SALES TAX	
SHIPPING (SEE BELOW)	
TOTAL	

No returns.
All prices subject to change without notice.

Bulk discounts available, please inquire.
All orders must be prepaid.

Phone orders accepted with MasterCard or Visa.
Call (802)247-3132 or fax (802)247-4233.

Make checks payable to: **SAFER SOCIETY PRESS**

www.safersociety.org

Mail to:

Safer Society Press
PO BOX 340 • BRANDON • VT • 05733
A program of The Safer Society Foundation, Inc.

Shipping and Handling

1–4 items	$5	21–25 items	$17
5–10 items	$8	26–30 items	$20
11–15 items	$12	31–35 items	$23
16–20 items	$14	36–40 items	$26
	41–50 items	$31	
	51+ items	call for quote	